THE
ORIGIN AND PROPERTIES
OF THE HUMAN AURA

By

OSCAR BAGNALL
B.A., Cantab

Foreword by

SIBYL FERGUSON

Illustrated

SAMUEL WEISER, INC.
York Beach, Maine

First Published in London 1937
This American Edition 1975

Reprinted 1981

Copyright © by Samuel Weiser, Inc. 1975

Samuel Weiser, Inc.
P.O. Box 612
York Beach, Maine 03910

ISBN 0-87728-284-6

Library of Congress Catalogue Card No. 74-84848

Printed in the U.S.A. by
Noble Offset Printers, Inc., New York, N.Y. 10003

CONTENTS

LIST OF ILLUSTRATIONS

FOREWORD

Since interest in the aura has more than re-doubled recently, it is appropriate to reissue Oscar Bagnall's THE ORIGIN AND PROPERTIES OF THE HUMAN AURA. Both scientific and occult groups are investigating the aura, which has been variously described as a radiation or emanation surrounding the physical body. Some claim an aura envelops all living beings, including animals and plants. A few inquirers believe inanimate objects, also, have a narrow emanation. Often those who see the aura differ regarding the width of the radiation, asserting it may extend from an inch to five feet or over.

Presumably the occultists were the first to discuss the aura and assign properties to it—some of which were highly extravagant. The pictures of saints and other divine persons with a nimbus about their heads intrigued them. Also they discovered the luminous haze surrounding these sacred images had been pictured by the ancients, antedating Christianity. Consequently, it was assumed that only spiritual people had halos, and only clairvoyants perceived this burden of light, and were able to interpret it. Since the clairvoyants received their gift from God, it was natural for them to see the aura. That the artists who painted the religious pictures were also gifted with second sight is questionable. In many cases the painter who depicted the phenomenon was anything but spiritual.

On the side of the scientists, there were the outstanding German, Baron Carl von Reichenbach who discovered the Odic force, and in America,

Dr. Edwin Babbit, who, in 1878, promulgated color and healing in his book, THE PRINCIPLES OF LIGHT AND COLOR.

The first scientific man to begin investigating the aura in a way acceptable to present-day scientists was Dr. Walter J. Kilner, a respected member of the staff of St. Thomas's Hospital in London. In 1879 he assumed charge of the Electro-Therapy Department, when this radically new venture in medicine was established.

Dr. Kilner was aware of the pictured nimbus, and considered it well worth investigating, for had not von Reichenbach and Babbit both made numerous attempts to accomplish this very thing. Dr. Kilner's story has been told in detail many times. It is enough to repeat that his experiments were successful to the extent that he recorded the results of his research in a book, THE HUMAN ATMOSPHERE* (the original title), which continues to be read avidly sixty-three years later.

Oscar Bagnall, as a young university man, read biology, chemistry and physics at Cambridge, finally taking his degree in science. Bagnall's studies led him to inquire into Dr. Kilner's experiments at St. Thomas's Hospital. He became involved in the experiments regarding the aura to such an extent, that after Dr. Kilner's death, Bagnall zealously carried on the scientific research himself. He pursued the investigation the remainder of his life, satisfied there is indeed a cloudy emanation surrounding the individual, which is a faithful indicator of bodily health.

Both Kilner and Bagnall disclaimed being clairvoyant, and regretted there was no other word for

*Published as THE AURA by Samuel Weiser Inc.

"aura". Their objective had been to prove the aura's value was diagnostic, a matter of scientific interest. They agreed the aura had nothing to do with spirituality. However, they did agree the emanations of a highly intelligent person are larger than those of an individual of low intelligence.

Some years ago a woman wrote to Bagnall, stating that she had seen auras all her life, and that an outstanding ophthalmogist had studied her eyes with intense interest. After exhaustive testing, he concluded she did see a luminous cloud about individuals. At this late date without access to the actual case history, it is remembered that the entire bit was laid to an unusual condition of the rods and cones, and an involvement with the ciliary muscle. The woman claimed this was more of an annoyance than a blessing. She emphatically believed that Kilner and Bagnall had seen the aura through the use of their aura-screen, as she saw it.

Once being privileged to speak to her, she was positive the aura is actually an attribute of the physical man. Everyone has a halo, even the most dissolute criminal. Often it is more positive than the "good" person's. After she discovered that not every body saw this seeming phenomenon, the woman spent her life trying to understand and describe it. She praised Kilner and Bagnall for their ability to place the aura before the public, stripping it of spiritual qualities and using it for diagnostic purposes. Reviewing all the claims regarding the appearance of the aura, she felt it was a matter of the "Emperor's Clothes".

If it were possible for Bagnall to take part in today's research, especially the work the Kirlians have accomplished, it would be worthwhile to get his reactions and his evaluation. The Kirlian experiments are a far cry from the simple screens developed by Kilner and Bagnall. In 1971 Ostrander and Schroeder discussed Kirlian photographs of a calm, healthy man's fingertips, and those of a tense, nervous man. The photographs differed appreciably, proving beyond doubt the sensitivity of the Kirlian technique. However, Bagnall in 1937 discussed the aura of a calm, healthy man, and the aura of a neurotic patient. Here, too, the evidence was conclusive, proving the accuracy of the Kilner and Bagnall screen. It is evident they were all working toward the same end. The pursuit of the aura has gone beyond theory into the realm of fact.

* * * * *

Sibyl Ferguson

THE ORIGIN AND PROPERTIES
OF THE HUMAN AURA

INTRODUCTION

IT is with some misgiving and not a little reticence that I take upon myself the task of producing a book dealing with the vexed subject of the haze that surrounds the living body.

It has been supposed for a long time that human beings are surrounded by something which has been called by the mystical name, the *aura* ; a name that has shrouded it in a veil of romance and fantasy almost to its ultimate exclusion as a subject for serious scientific research.

Videre est credere has been for ever the cry of the sceptical, and since the aura—I use the word for want of a better—has been most difficult, well-nigh impossible, to see hitherto, but few have troubled themselves further about it.

Many men of science will, however, admit

the possibility of its presence ; some will agree that this is a likelihood rather than a mere possibility. I believe I am right, though, in saying that the only work of note that has been published dealing with the subject as a whole from a scientific angle was that of Dr. Walter Kilner, an X-ray specialist who has been dead now for some years. He claimed to have seen the aura, to have examined it in much detail and to have made use of its appearance as an aid to diagnosing disease. His book is, in the main, a collection of his interesting cases, most of which date back to pre-war days. Since his death the matter has, at least so far as publications are concerned, been left in abeyance, though much has been written about it by those who are interested in the occult.

It is my intention to submit some properties that I consider to belong to the aura, and which I shall back up by scientific experimental evidence. The results of these experiments I have proved to my own satisfaction to be correct and I shall treat them, therefore, as facts. They shall be my data. Perchance my research may dovetail in with the theories of others and so provide some common ground for mutual advance along hitherto untrodden paths.

It is some years ago now since I first started

experimenting. I was interested in coloured screens and their effects on the retina with regard to colour blindness. I experienced much difficulty in obtaining a pure blue dye, for these seemed to have been a monopoly of the Germans. At last, comparatively recently, I managed to make up a satisfactory blue screen, and after I had been using it I discovered two interesting facts.

The first I think will appeal to some whose interest in this subject may be in other respects but lukewarm. It came about in quite a matter-of-fact way. It was in the summer time and I had got up early so as to put in several hours' work with my screens before eleven o'clock, when I was due to play cricket.

I should mention that I have lately moved over to the wrong side of forty and, perhaps on account of my having used my microscope more than I ought to have done, I have discovered that my eyes are just beginning to find some difficulty in negotiating nearer objects. On this particular occasion I had asked to be left out of the side, as I had much work to do and the match was a two-days' one. However, the inevitable happened. I was roped in to play. We lost the toss and I found myself crouching down behind the stumps when an hour earlier I had sensitized my eyes to see hyper-short waves. The first few overs were fast, straight stuff and all went well, but I was doubtful as to what I should be like when the spin bowlers came on. I received the surprise of my life. A real good one. That day I saw every ball right into my gloves. My sight had become young again. The second discovery I sought deliberately in order to confirm the truth of the first. I tried the effect on the focus of my microscope, and sure enough I got the confirmation that I wanted.

When I used the instrument with my eyes sensitized I always had to alter the focus that had suited my unsensitized retina. The alteration was a considerable one of the coarse adjustment.

Thoroughly pleased with my new sight I, of course, set to work to consider the cause. It occurred to me that I might possibly be able to see rays with ultra-short wave-lengths, and so experimented with different types of light. At length I managed to see a haze surrounding the human body.

Presuming this haze to consist, at least for the most part, of waves of a length shorter than that of visible light, it was clear that these rays would become visible only when a change

4

had been produced upon the eye's retina, the result of which change being to sensitize it to wave-lengths slightly shorter than it can appreciate normally.

Since the aura cannot be seen in complete darkness, it follows that the body does not emit rays in sufficient quantity to stimulate the sense of vision.

It is impossible to make any hard and fast statement regarding the amount of light necessary or the most helpful colour for a background. These are questions that each observer must answer for himself, using his personal experience alone to guide him. Most people prefer a room darkened by heavy curtains so that daylight is diffused through them. It is a help to have black serge blinds, one on a roller at the top of the window to pull down, and another on a roller at the bottom of the window to pull up. In this way one can have a double thickness if required.

The subject under observation should stand on the other side of the room, facing the window. The background that the majority prefer is either a black or a dark red one.

For my own part I like the room not too dark. I also prefer a lighter background than most.

The light must be regulated to suit the observer and also the conditions. As a general rule a good day for taking photographs is a good day for inspecting the aura, but this rule by no means applies invariably. You cannot say with any degree of certainty that a particular day will be no good for seeing the aura, any more than when out hunting you can say there will be no scent. One of the hottest scents I remember was travelling waist-high along the side of a stream on a day when there seemed to be no humidity in the air whatsoever. So, too, I have seen the aura very clearly indeed in a thunderstorm.

This aura surrounding the body has been referred to often as resembling a halo. I always associate a halo with part of the uniform of a saint—something unreal and " pictured strange in musty unread book." The haze with which I intend to deal is no saintly decoration, but shines forth alike both from the just and the unjust, its quality being influenced, I feel, rather by health and by mental ability than by any factor that shall be accounted unto it for righteousness.

Again, the auric haze has been confused with the supernatural in general and with ghosts in particular. Clearly nothing of the sort can be emitted by a body unless the body be present to emit it. Even the Executioner to the Queen of Hearts would admit the logic of this.

Let me say here that this is not intended to refer in any way to inter-communication between those amongst us and those who have passed on. I have never attempted to get into touch with the dead, and such being the case, it would, to say the least of it, be in poor taste to decry this. I define the word "aura," as I use it, as being simply a haze emitted by the living body. I hope to show what it is and even to suggest the parts of the body from which it has its origin. There is as yet insufficient data to hand to justify any definite deduction as to where *exactly* it has its source. But there is much evidence that is, to say the least of it, significant. "Knowledge brings doubts and exceptions and limitations, which are all hindrances to vigorous statement."

CHAPTER I

THE APPEARANCE OF THE NORMAL AURA

LET me begin by dealing with the aura as it appears to me. I refer to the aura in general, the average aura of a healthy person.

In the neighbourhood of the skin and extending from it for some three inches there is a brighter aura which appears to be more solid than that beyond it. It seems to be made up of lines very close together, running directly away from the body. It hugs the body fairly closely—I mean by this that it is of much the same shape as the body, only extended a few inches beyond it on either side. I am presuming that the subject being inspected is standing facing the observer.

This inside aura varies in brightness directly as the health of its owner. Extending some six to eight inches beyond this again is an outer haze which gradually fades away at its distal margin, but which is more or less oval in shape.

It has been claimed that the colour of this will vary. Some say that the aura can be red, gold, brown, all sorts of colours, dependent upon the character of the person emitting it. I am not going to contradict this, of course.

Personally I have seen nothing like it. The aura, this outer haze, has always been misty, pale blue to pale grey. The better the intellect of the subject, the bluer the haze.

The inside aura is much the same in appearance in all of us—men, women and children. Not so the outer haze. Up to the age of puberty it protrudes only some four inches beyond the brighter inside aura. From about the age of fourteen up to eighteen a woman's aura gradually widens until it attains about eight inches (nearly a foot in all), becoming oval, the widest part being about the waist-line.

This widening does not take place in the aura of a man, and for this reason women prove the more satisfactory subjects.

The inside part of the aura has always been distinctly brighter than the haze beyond it and there is, to me, a fairly clear boundary between them. One must not conclude, though, as soon as the eyes have been temporarily sensitized by the screen for the first time, that

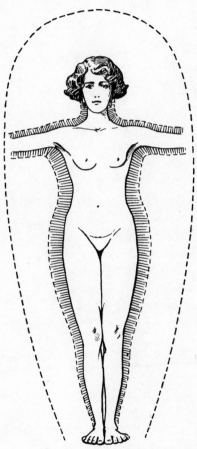

Woman, normal aura.

each of one's fellow-beings is going to appear surrounded by a dazzling halo which in turn will be bathed in a kind of sunset effect. This quite decidedly never happens.

Having gazed at the sky, not at the sun direct, through a dark dicyanin screen for a minute or two, next cast the eyes around, still keeping the screen in place. The foliage appears a plum colour and soon seems to become hazy. Care should be taken before affixing the screen to see that the glasses are dry and that all moisture is removed from the face in the neighbourhood of the eyes. The mistiness which would thus be caused. is not entirely unlike the haze when it first begins to appear.

Next examine the hands. It seems as if steam is rising from them. Place the tips of the fingers of the one hand against the tips of the corresponding ones of the other. Then draw them slowly apart. The lines should be observed running from finger to finger.

It may occur to some of my readers that this is simply an optical illusion, the lines appearing to remain in the path travelled by the fingers. This suspicion, however, can easily be set at rest. If the hands are drawn apart aslant— e.g. by pushing the left hand away and drawing the right towards the body, as shown in the

13

diagram, it will be found that the connecting lines run diagonally also.

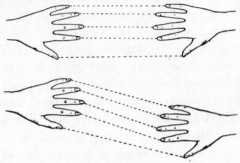

Rays between the fingers.

Again, one cannot make these lines curve; they are always straight lines.

Rays of light travel in straight lines. Ultra-violet rays must do so, too, *a fortiori*.

Notice also that the haze extends further around the tips of the fingers than around their shanks.

It is unlikely that more than this will be seen at the first attempt, for the action of the dye is cumulative. Later on it will be found that, having sensitized the eyes for some two or three minutes as described, one can dispense with the screen, or at least replace it by a much weaker one, and that the aura will remain visible for some considerable time afterwards, the length of time depending on the accumulation acquired, and also to some extent upon the eyes. Some people see the aura much more clearly as well as more quickly than others do. The description of the aura, which will occupy the greater part of this chapter, is an attempt to explain in detail its component parts as they have appeared to me, and to several others, under ideal conditions. Variations in weather conditions will naturally make some difference both to the material part of the aura as well as to the absorption of its ultra-violet rays. Changes of temperature, treated purely as such, have no influence so far as I have been able to discover.

The brighter inside aura appears, as I have said, to follow the outline of the body, extending from it some three inches. It seems to be made up of a number of small rays (as undoubtedly it is) running parallel to one another and at right angles to the body.

Sometimes longer, and still brighter, pencils of rays extend from the proximal edge of this aura beyond it so as to encroach upon, or possibly to extend beyond, the outer haze. These rays, of course, travel in straight lines though not necessarily parallel to those of the aura.

They are in all probability of the same origin as the aura and have been seen to run towards some prominent object in the proximity of the body, even an inanimate object, such as the pole of a bar magnet.

These rays may be observed stretching from one part (probably from a projection) of the body to another—for example, when the hands are raised above the head rays may be seen to extend beyond the inside aura both from the head and from the arm, and to link together in the space between so as to make a continuous pencil of rays from head to arm. Because the rays from the head are somewhat brighter than those from the arms, the pencils have the appearance of running from head to arms.

The whole phenomenon is possibly a kind of auric attraction in such a case. Occasionally such bundles of rays have been noticed extending through the outer haze and out beyond, heading nowhere in particular. These rays, too, are brighter than the rest of the inside aura. Imagine oneself looking down from a cliff on to a sea front along which is a row of bright lamps throwing a gleam out into the water. The sea front corresponds to the skin, the gleam of the lamps to the inside aura. A strong searchlight throwing its beam across the sea, not necessarily at right angles to the sea front, possibly diagonally, would well represent this stronger bundle of rays.

These rays must be either given out by some part of the body, differing from the rest of the auric emission for some specific reason, or drawn away from it by some external attracting force. I incline to the latter view. If this is the case, it means that the inside aura is sufficiently elastic to allow these flagella-like rays to be drawn out to some three times their natural visible length. The obvious drawback to this view lies in the fact that it does not satisfactorily account for the additional brightness of such rays when compared with the rest of the aura.

In order that I might the more easily examine one of the constituent parts of the aura, it has been necessary to dim the other in an attempt to exclude its influence.

If the aura is examined through a *red* screen the outer haze becomes less obvious, and so a better estimate can be formed as to the exact distal margin of the inside aura.

This experiment is not possible, of course, until one's eyes have reached that stage of accumulation where the aura can be seen after the removal of the dicyanin screen.

I have found, too, that a *blue* screen tends :

1. To make the distal margin of the outer haze much more obvious;
2. to make the inside aura look more bright though less sharply defined.

I find that this screen is tending, not so much to obliterate the inside aura as to intensify the outer which I believe to lie beneath it, or, rather, to be intermingling with it.

The outer haze, I consider, originates partly from the skin and so will run through the inside aura beyond which it extends.

Perhaps I ought to say that this opinion is entirely contrary to that of others, and so to the generally accepted one, so far as there are any accepted opinions in what is, comparatively speaking, an uncharted sea of scientific research.

I have noticed a blank space, a void, between the skin and the inside aura. It has the appearance of a dark band and is not more than an eighth of an inch in width.

Dr. Kilner—who was perhaps the first pioneer to experiment on really scientific lines with the aura—claims that this void is always present. He called it the Etheric Double, and treated it as a possible third constituent part of the whole aura. He even went so far as to say that it appeared to him to be very slightly pink tinted.

I feel, however, that very few of us indeed can hope to see what Dr. Kilner saw, for he was undoubtedly singularly gifted in this respect—clairvoyant. I have tested most of his claims and I have found that I can vouch for the majority of them from my own personal experience. Others, however, I do not for one moment presume to doubt, though I have never been able to confirm them, because my eyes can see no further beyond the violet than anybody's else, except, of course, artificially.

I certainly think that what I have seen, others can see too, provided that they have average sight. I am convinced that clairvoyance, like hands in a horseman or wrists in a batsman, is a gift of the gods, and cannot be acquired to any very marked degree. Dicyanin does give one a good lift along the road into the ultra-violet, however. I tell you everything I can, like the White Knight, and really there is little enough to relate, for I am determined to set down only what I have seen.

Let us now turn our attention to the outer haze—mystical, a thing of moods, changeable as Proteus, and teeming with possibilities. *Præter opiniones* I cannot think of this haze as

19

beginning where the inside aura leaves off. It, too, is clearly emitted from some source within the body.

Examined through a blue screen—Kilner used methylene blue—I prefer a mixture containing blue pinacyanol which acts as a sensitizing screen at the same time—so as to intensify it, and thus obscure the inner aura by comparison (it is as a general rule difficult to dim this part of the aura without obliterating the outer haze as well), it will be noticed that the inside aura seems less striated, taking on more of the misty appearance of the outer haze. It will be remembered that the inside aura appears as parallel rays running outwards from, and at right angles to, the skin, while the outer haze is misty rather than striped. Clearly, then, since the outer haze has been intensified and the usually brighter inside aura by comparison dimmed, it is fair to infer that one is viewing the outer haze running through the inside aura, and to presume that it, too, emanates from the skin.

The distal margin is nothing hard and fast, but the haze can certainly be considered as having a definite shape. In children of either sex, and also in men, the haze is comparatively narrow and possibly brighter than it is in the case of women, for it seems to be closer knit, compressed, following more or less the shape of the body, only to a lesser degree than does the inside aura. Males and children, therefore, make uninteresting subjects for the examination of this haze, and my remarks will apply in particular to the much wider haze that can be seen surrounding a woman. The shape is roughly oval, being widest at the waist-line and tapering gradually towards the ankles. The haze is less compact than it is in the case of a man, the distal edge is less clearly defined. Uncertain, a thing unleashed, groping away into space. Indefinite, it is true, but tremendously interesting.

May I emphasize that I have found nothing whatever to suggest that *this haze* could possibly represent an electric field around the body ; it does not seem to be material, that is to say, it has no appreciable mass. There can be little doubt in my mind that it consists of rays the wave-length of which is not, under normal conditions, visible to the human eye.

Just as a horse's coat or a dog's nose gives one an indication as to physical condition, so, too, the inside aura changes, being brighter and sharper in outline when a person is in robust health. In like manner the outer haze may be said to register mental capacity. As mentioned before, the only colour I have ever seen imparted to the haze, disregarding pathological cases, has varied from pale blue to pale grey. The bluer and the finer the haze, the better the intellect—that is the general rule. If a body emits a haze that is grey and dull, it almost certainly houses wits that are dull also.

Grey hazes vary in shades of grey from the blue-grey to the drab grey, almost brown-tinted grey, of the negro.

The haze surrounding a very young baby is rather greeny, with very little differentiation between the inside and outer parts of the aura.

It is very difficult to determine the exact point in life when one becomes possessed of an aura—it is certainly considerably earlier than birth. Newly born babies always have an aura, though it is not always very obvious without suitable background. The widening of the aura of a pregnant woman, particularly as the time of birth approaches, I have suggested in a later chapter, may be due to her aura's being augmented by that of the unborn baby. Often, too, her aura is brighter over the abdominal region as well as wider. The Law rules that life begins at birth. Biology has proved that conception marks our beginning ; for the zygote nucleus in the original cell undoubtedly lives and equally undoubtedly is created by both male and female, as can be demonstrated by following the division of the micro-nucleus in an animal as elementary even as the unicellular paramœcium.

Women who are mothers speak of their babies having come to life, or quickened, at a particular time during the period of pregnancy, usually about three months after conception. The wider aura has been noticed as being permanently present as early as that. The widening seen at the beginning of pregnancy is not permanent and cannot be attributable to the formation of the aura of the embryo since it occurs also with the onset of menstruation, as has been described in detail, too, in the chapter dealing with the aura in connexion with sex.

I feel that the aura is emitted at this point, namely six months before birth, though the question of the embryo aura must necessarily entail more guesswork than scientific argument can safely carry. If it is emitted then, why should it not be emitted earlier in life, even from the moment of conception ? My own impression is that all living things emit an aura, though just where in the solar spectrum the wave-lengths of the component rays lie in the

23

various creatures—and so the possibility of their becoming visible to the human eye—it has as yet been impossible to find out. I have been concentrating my research only upon rendering visible auric rays whose wave-length is just a little shorter than that of the violet end of the visible spectrum. The aura emitted by the human embryo in the early days after conception, if such an aura be emitted, would surely be made up of ultra-violet rays—I do not see that any form of metamorphosis can alter the wave-length—but an aura so feeble as this must necessarily be would not be made visible by screens in their present state of comparative imperfection.

The beginning thus corresponds more or less to the beginning of life, and the intensity increases gradually as the embryo gains in size and strength. The aura persists as long as life lasts, and seems to cease to be emitted the moment that death has taken place.

While there is an aura there is life—and, presumably, as soon as there is life there will be an aura emitted.

Until the screens have been improved so as to render the eye vastly more sensitive to ultra-violet rays, it will be impossible to settle the question. There must be sensitizers eminently more suitable to our purpose than the mixture I am using in my screens at present. They need finding, which will entail infinite research —and expense.

When something better has been discovered, we may learn something further with regard to the " atmosphere " that surrounds us.

CHAPTER II

PHYSICAL PROPERTIES

MAY I again dispel the suggestion that the aura is something mysterious, becoming visible only to the favoured few who attribute to it psychic powers for which they fail to offer any scientific support.

Where the body is, there will the haze emitted by it be also. If we are unable to see it, it is our own eyes which must receive our attention, for clearly we cannot change the atmosphere that surrounds the bodies of others. That this haze, or aura, is physical fact and not existing only in the imagination as an optical illusion of subjective nature I will endeavour to prove.

I contend, too, that by artificial means which I will describe in detail the aura can be seen, not only by the few, but by the majority of people with normal sight, and I will explain in full tests that I have made in order to ascertain its physical properties.

26

Firstly, I have already suggested that the aura is emitted by the living body only.

A haze can be seen surrounding a newly born baby—I have seen it a few hours after birth. It remains throughout life and can be seen around people of any age.

No aura is emitted after death has taken place. Although I have had no opportunity of inspecting a corpse immediately following death, I have no doubt that the aura vanishes at the same moment that death takes place. Faintness on the part of the subject undergoing inspection causes the aura to fade, and the return of consciousness brings it back gradually.

I presume that animals, too, emit auras, but I have been unable to recognize one with any certainty from the smaller animals that I have used as subjects. It seems extremely probable that their auras are visible to other animals. Here is an interesting experiment :

An owl can see mice from a considerable distance in the dark.

This bird will give a very good account of himself against a much larger animal, should one approach him at night, yet he is helpless in the daylight.

Of course, we know that he has specially

night-sensitized eyes, but I have found that an owl could not locate a piece of *dead meat* even at night, although he showed clearly that he was hungry.

The inference, surely, is that the owl sees the live mouse because the mouse's body emits rays which are interpreted as visible light to the eyes of the owl, thereby causing it to stand out against the dark background.

A theory often put forward accredits the bird with hearing far superior to his feathered neighbours'. The obvious objection to this is the fact that the owl's power in this direction is so much more pronounced at night.

That of attributing it to light emitted by the hapless prey is, to my mind, very much nearer the mark.

Have you ever stood at night and watched the eyes of animals in the bush and tried to guess what they are? We can see only their eyes, and have little but the colour to help us ; perhaps they can see a great deal more of us.

Now I come to my second point : I suggest that the aura is an ultra-violet phenomenon. I might call it ultra-violet *light* except that one cannot normally see these rays.

Just as our ears are capable of appreciating

only wave-lengths between a certain range—waves that give us sensations of sound have a frequency between 30 and 38,000—so our eyes are capable of translating into visible light only waves whose lengths cover a limited range. The person who can hear anything higher (i.e. of shorter wave-length) than the squeak—it appears to our ears as a squeak—of a bat must be rare, though no doubt some of the smaller animals have a cry which we cannot appreciate as sound ; in other words, which we are unable to hear. So, too, with sight : the longest waves that we can see we call red light, the next longest give us orange, then yellow, green, blue, indigo and lastly violet, the shortest. These are the colours of the visible spectrum. Rays of wave-length shorter than those that we see as violet light we term ultra-violet, since, being unable to see them, we do not know what colour they are. I suggest that the aura consists of, or certainly contains, ultra-violet rays.

The lens of our eye changes its curvature as the object we are looking at approaches nearer to or recedes further from us, so that the image of that object is formed exactly on the retina. Since the red rays bend less than the violet ones, both will not be focused exactly on the retina. Yellow usually appears as the brightest colour in the spectrum, so let us imagine that the yellow rays are focused exactly on the retina, the red ones very slightly behind and the violet ones a trifle short, or in front of it. If we can manage to sensitize our eyes to see slightly shorter rays, making, let us say, the blue rays focus exactly on the retina, then the violet ones will have become more nearly into exact focus, and so brighter, while we may thus become enabled to see into the ultra-violet.

If this can be done—and I will describe how I personally have found that it can in a subsequent chapter—the obvious question arises : What has happened to our eyes to bring about this change ?

Here are some of the possibilities :

1. An increase in curvature of the lens or, perhaps, of the cornea. Surely there would hardly be time for that ?

2. An increase of the solids in solution in, say, the vitreous humour sufficient to alter its refractive index. This, too, seems impossible, though perhaps the same result could be brought about by some chemical change in the substance.

The aura given off by the body, which I believe to consist of rays of ultra-violet wavelength, appears as a mist, or haze ; the lens and the vitreous humour being albuminous bodies fluoresce, receiving the ultra-violet rays and emitting them as light. This light does not stimulate the cones of the retina, but rods perceive it in the form of a blue-grey mist. Here, I feel, we may have part of the answer.

By systematically sensitizing my eyes this effect can be reached. There seems but little doubt that the influence is being exerted upon the nervous system of the eyes.

It was Kilner again who claimed that he had brought about a satisfactory sensitizing of the eyes by the use of screens containing an alcoholized solution of dicyanin, one of the coaltar products.

I, too, have used a modification of this method with success, though whether the effect is *entirely* due to the sensitizing properties of dicyanin or in some small measure to the production of a temporary colour blindness due to the colour peculiar to the solution is a moot point. Blue glass alone is quite useless, of course. However, more of this later on.

I enter upon my third point with an appropriate degree of reticence ; since nobody else has advanced it, I expect disagreement on this point.

Diseased organs emit a very faint aura, if any. Complaints of the alimentary canal or of the digestive glands affect the *inside* aura.

Puberty, menstruation, pregnancy and lactation are registered upon the *outer* haze ; so are intellect and nervous complaints.

Now, admitting the correctness of Darwin's theory of evolution, let us go back to early days when the most advanced animals had reached a stage somewhat similar to that reached by the earthworm to-day : the worm may be said to consist roughly of two cylinders, one inside the other.

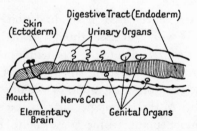

Section through earthworm showing the urinary and the genital organs situated in mesoderm, i.e. between the skin and the digestive tract.

The outer one is the skin (ectoderm) and the inner one the alimentary canal or digestive tract (endoderm). In between, in the mesoderm, the urino-genital organs are situated.

We, as individuals, pass through the stages of evolution between conception and birth. What took millions of years to come about is recapitulated in a few days.

Let us see what parts of us develop from which layers :

The ectoderm produces the skin and the nervous system.

The mesoderm, the urinary and the reproductive organs, among others.

The endoderm gives rise to the walls of the alimentary canal and the glands opening into the canal.

The outer haze is affected by nervous disorders and by changes due to sex.

The inside aura registers diseases of the alimentary canal and its glands—among other things—and ill-health in general.

I submit that the comparison is, at least, significant !

Next let us examine briefly the effect of outside forces upon the aura.

The first question that suggests itself to my

mind is, perhaps : " Is it a vapour ? " The answer must be " No." It is not affected by change of temperature, neither can it be dispersed by a current of air.

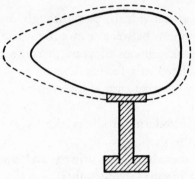

Electric field around a charged conductor.

Again : " Is it made up of electrically charged particles ? " A much more difficult question. Rays are not material. Magnets cannot have any effect on a haze unless it has some mass, such as particles carrying a charge would have. Psychic people tell me that magnets attract the aura, or repel it. I have never been able to make the slightest impression upon the *outer haze* with a bar magnet, a horse-shoe magnet, an electro-magnet or any other sort of magnet—but the inside aura has " run to " a magnet if placed close enough. On

34

presenting the other pole the same thing happened. Therefore, it seems that the inside aura may be magnetizable, but that it has no polarity.

Electric field around a charged rod.

Another fact that points, to some extent, the same way : the aura extends farther from a projection, such as the point of a finger or the

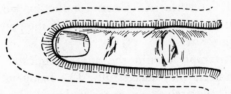

Aura around a finger.

nipple of a breast, than it does from a flatter surface. So does the field of an electrically charged conductor. If the inside aura may be considered as our electric field, the outer haze certainly is not. It seems that they arise from totally different sources. The sifting out of evidence on this point needs a chapter to itself. Let me say this now, though : If the subject be placed upon an insulated stand and be treated with an electric charge from a Wimshurst machine, the *inside* aura will vanish, but after some minutes will gradually return much expanded. Others have said that if the charge is continued the outside haze will contract. I have not found that electricity makes any difference to the size of this haze at all.

It will no doubt occur to electricians that some bodies are drier than others. Unless the skin is damp it does not conduct electricity very well. I had allowed for that when making observations with regard to the field off points and flat surfaces. Good conducting surfaces must be used if one is to show that the potential is thus varied.

Attempts to tint the aura chemically have not been very successful. The halogens suggest themselves at once as being the most promising. Iodine vapour is heavy and might, I thought, be poured down the side of the body. The vapour could be seen, but precious little aura! Iodine is, of course, a dark purple solid and, if heated, passes straight into a vapour, there being no liquid state. This property makes it convenient for our purpose— nothing messy. I determined to try again. Making as much as would pass down between the clothing and the skin, I fumigated the clothing with the vapour. On examining the aura a little later it appeared, on that side of the body only, to be slightly brown. A failure, I think, as the skin had probably absorbed some of the vapour, thus colouring the aura, very slightly, only indirectly. Bromine is less pleasant. It is a brown liquid, becoming on being heated a brown vapour. The result was somewhat similar, only to a lesser degree. Bromine is not so heavy as iodine.

I have tried ammonia, thinking that I might be able to judge the better whether the aura could be affected directly. Ammonia is not coloured, so I imagined that any change in colour that might be observed would be due to auric change and not to the presence of vapour hanging around the skin. However, I saw nothing worthy of note.

I have often been asked whether there is any possibility of the aura's being due to radioactivity. The only elements that are radioactive to any marked degree all have high atomic weights. The heaviest element that is present in our bodies in an appreciable quantity is iron, the atomic weight of which is only 56. This fact alone negatives the possibility of radio-activity quite conclusively, to my mind.

Lastly, it has been claimed that when the

auras of two individuals meet, attraction or repulsion takes place. This has been given as a reason for one's taking an instant liking or dislike to a person that one meets for the first time.

It *has* been suggested to me that the woman's extra-wide aura would account for her gift of intuition.

I cannot agree that the *outer* hazes either attract or repel one another.

The inside auras do appear to run together, it is true, but it is not often that the *inside* auras of two individuals approach one another sufficiently closely at a first meeting for them to express their mutual likes or dislikes.

I realize that their respective auras would come into contact with one another during a hand-shake. Personally, I cannot claim to have gleaned much information from shaking hands. Try, the next time you grasp a mitt. If you expect nothing, then you will not be disappointed.

CHAPTER III

APPARATUS AND HOW TO USE IT

LET us presume that the aura, at least for the most part, consists of rays the wave-lengths of which are shorter than those of visible light ; that they are ultra-violet.

These rays, then, will become visible only when a change has been produced upon the eye's retina, the result of which change being to sensitize it to wave-lengths slightly shorter than it can appreciate normally.

Since the aura cannot be seen in complete darkness it follows that it does not emit rays in sufficient quantity to stimulate a sense of vision, at any rate upon the cones of the retina.

Very many of the sun's rays never reach the earth. Some are absorbed by the envelope of gas that surrounds the sun itself, others are lost on entering the earth's atmosphere. Of those that do reach us the majority we are unable to see. The visible spectrum stretches from the red limit where the wave-length is about

800-millionths of 1 mm. to the violet limit with a wave-length of 400-millionths.

The rays that lie beyond the red possess a large amount of energy, as can be illustrated by their warming effect. The ultra-violet rays have a very short wave-length and a greater refrangibility. Although we cannot see these ultra-violet rays under normal conditions their presence can be shown by the fact that certain silver salts are affected by them—they are the photographic rays, sometimes spoken of as the *actinic* rays.

Since the ultra-violet rays are more refrangible than those in the visible spectrum, it follows that they will be the more readily absorbed on passing through denser media, such as glass, than through air. We have already said that our atmosphere absorbs some rays ; *a fortiori* denser media such as the lens of the eye and the vitreous humour must absorb even longer rays. Professor Starling says that an eye, the lens of which had been removed for cataract, had its wave-length appreciation increased on the violet side from 397 to 313. Thus it is evident that the lens alone absorbs rays of the utmost importance from our point of view, namely, in dealing with the aura.

As regards density of media : clearly the farther above sea-level, the thinner the air— and so, the better, a vacuum being ideal. Water has a refractive index of $\frac{4}{3}$ as compared with that of glass which is $\frac{3}{2}$. Crown glass is better than flint, and quartz is better than either.

Next I come to the question of screens and their preparation. Two pieces of flat glass cemented together some 3 to 5 mm. apart— the exact distance apart will, of course, depend on the strength of the solution. The glass should be thin, obviously, so as to avoid refraction. Dicyanin is a coal-tar dye and is difficult to obtain in this country in reasonably small quantities—mine has had to be got from Germany. The substance has isomerides ; that is to say, the atoms which make it up will link together differently in each kind, though the number of atoms of each element present in the molecule will be the same in each case. These isomerides are called dicyanin A, dicyanin B. It does not matter a great deal which is used.

The substance is insoluble in water so has to be dissolved in alcohol or, better still, bought ready as an alcoholized solution.

The screen should be filled with this and then

sealed up. This is important for at least three reasons :

1. The alcohol evaporates quickly ;
2. the dye deteriorates if exposed to the atmosphere, especially if it gets warm ;
3. it is dangerous stuff to get into your skin.

The solution should be dark bluey violet in colour, not green.

No light must reach the eyes except through the screen while the eyes are being sensitized.

Lenses mounted in the form of collapsible goggles made of some black material to keep out the light I have found as satisfactory as anything. The goggles fasten behind the head by means of elastic.

The lenses will, of course, be hollow so that they can be filled with dicyanin. They can also be slightly curved, concave or convex, to suit the eye.

No matter what kind of screen is used, the sensitizing process consists of gazing at the sky, not at the sun direct, through this dark dicyanin screen for perhaps a couple of minutes —which should be quite long enough ; it is possible to overdo this, bringing about fatigue, in which case one must wait until the eyes have recovered.

Having looked at the sky, lower the eyes and examine the surrounding foliage. Next try drawing the fingers apart as described in Chapter I. I do not recommend the use of full-length subjects in the first instance. Being able to distinguish anything other than a blur, perhaps, will not come for some time. Those who pick up a screen for the first time and expect the sun to be darkened and the moon to refuse to give her light are doomed to disappointment. The dye's power is cumulative and gradual. Better results in all probability will be obtained if the screen is not removed at first until the action of the dye upon the eye has accumulated sufficiently to enable the aura to become visible after the screen has been removed.

Half-way measures give, perhaps, the best results of all : after gazing through the dark screen to sensitize the retina, replace it by a lighter screen, i.e. one containing a weaker solution of dicyanin.

If you see nothing at first, do not strain your eyes by *staring* too hard. Just *look* naturally—and wait.

Do not use the screens for too long at a sitting. It is a great temptation, I know ; particularly when you are seeing very well.

43

But eye strain would mean your being able to do no more of this work until the eyes had recovered.

If nothing can be seen after using the screen for several minutes, a more, or a less, subdued light should be tried. When the appropriate light for the particular eye in question has been discovered, one should certainly see what appears to be a mist around the fingers. No two people like quite the same light. I can see nothing in a dark corner with heavy curtains drawn around me. My eyes take a good deal of sensitizing. Others have said that they can still see rays extending from the fingers even an hour after the screen has been laid aside, and this sometimes at the first attempt, too. Such people, however, have invariably been young and have had excellent sight.

One must not expect to be able to differentiate between the inside aura and the haze beyond it at the first sitting, nor, indeed, until the cumulative action of the dye has thoroughly sensitized the eyes—acclimatized them, so to speak, to see the aura without effort. This must of necessity be a gradual process.

The mist seen, as I have said, appears to be of a blue-grey colour. The point that next arises is whether this bluish colour is due to waves of the length that is normally responsible for producing the colour we call blue, or whether they are of a length shorter than that which we can see as violet, the last colour at the short-wave end of the visible spectrum.

If the colour is produced by the reflection of rays of light of a wave-length giving the colour blue, then one would expect the colour to be changed to the usual shades when looked at through coloured glass. The colours are not the ones that they ought to be. It seems, therefore, that this colour is perhaps the next colour beyond violet ; that is to say it is produced by wave-lengths shorter than those that give us violet light and which are usually spoken of as being of ultra-violet red length. The suggestion is, then, that ultra-violet red, the " colour " that we cannot normally see and which comes next beyond violet, is this grey-blue shade. Let us call it lavender.

This lavender is the usual colour of the aura, particularly of the outer haze. I have mentioned that sometimes it is rather bluer, and sometimes rather more grey—also that the better developed the mental capacity of the subject, the bluer the haze. Perhaps the rays producing the bluer lavender are of a slightly different wave-length than those responsible for the greyer colour.

There is, however, another side to this question. I think it probable that the aura does not exert sufficient effect upon the cones of the retina to produce any great degree of stimulation of the fovea centralis. The rods always see things in one colour—grey. I shall deal with this point more fully in a later chapter.

It is, of course, possible—even probable—that dyes other than dicyanin have the same effect upon the nerves of the retina—I have got good results from pinacyanol. The necessary qualification is that it should be of a blue or a violet colour ; one that will transmit the shorter wave-lengths of the spectrum. In fact, it should bring the object slightly nearer to the eye.

If, after gazing at the light for a minute or so through a screen containing a solution of a particular dye, one finds that it does this, then it has indeed distinct possibilities. The microscope must decide.

Get some very small, thin object, such as a fly's leg, into focus. If, after looking through the dye, one finds that it is still in focus, then the chances are that the right dye has not been discovered.

46

If, however, the coarse adjustment screw has to be turned appreciably so as to bring the object glass nearer to the slide, then it is clear that the dye under observation has the all-important property in common with dicyanin.

As regards the apparatus, it should be remembered that glass cuts out ultra-violet rays almost entirely. Quartz cells can be used for filters. It is most difficult to hit upon a really suitable substance that will absorb the rays of the visible spectrum and yet transmit ultra-violet ones.

May I say a word or two about the general use of filters ; for example, the Wratten filters which consist of two sets of coloured filters made in gelatine. The first set is of the primary colours, blue, green and red, and these let through one-third of the spectrum each. The second set are of the three complementary colours, peacock blue, magenta and yellow, each of which lets through a different two-thirds of the spectrum. When pairs of these complementaries are combined they give the three primaries, all three complementaries giving black.

There are two words, before closing this chapter, which no doubt will come to mind, namely *fluorescence* and *phosphorescence*. Their exact meanings—and difference—may not be clear to all.

Fluorescence : Suppose a spectrum falls upon a barium platinocyanide screen, violet will shine green. So will ultra-violet. The screen absorbs the energy of these rays, and emits it again in the form of green light. The name fluorescence is taken from the first substance to be used for this purpose, fluorspar, by Stokes, over three-quarters of a century ago. Quinine Sulphate has this power, too, and so have several other substances. They bring about a change of wave-length in the rays they absorb before re-emitting them.

Phosphorescence : There are substances which, if they are exposed to the light, will themselves give out light when placed in the dark, though normally they would be classified as non-luminous bodies. The most active rays in causing phosphorescence are the violet and those of shorter wave-length still.

Phosphorus has a pale green luminous appearance when exposed to moist air in the absence of light. This is due to slow combustion on the part of the phosphorus ; a chemical change which if exposed to light does not become reversible. Phosphorus is not truly phosphorescent. Calcium Sulphide can be made to shine in the dark for several hours after being exposed to bright sunlight. This is phosphorescence since the light from the sun gives the substance an energy which it in turn gives out in the dark. If again exposed to the sunlight it will once more become phosphorescent.

Fluorescent substances, on the other hand, will give out light only while the light is acting upon them. The most noticeable feature in fluorescence seems to be the fact that the colour, or rays, absorbed are nearly always of shorter wave-length than the colour re-emitted. The violet and ultra-violet can be absorbed to be given out fluorescently as green. Although we cannot use this phenomenon very easily to enable us to see ultra-violet rays, as such, it is clear that we can absorb these ultra-short waved rays so that they may be re-emitted as visible light. In short, the presence of ultra-violet rays in any particular case can be established through fluorescence, though they cannot be seen as ultra-violet.

As I have said, I have found dicyanin a most useful substance ; possible other coal-tar dyes will come to light where this property is concerned. My present screens contain very little dicyanin.

Among the other fluorescent substances, apart from platino-cyanide of barium which has this property of fluorescence to a more pronounced degree than the rest, are quinine which is colourless and fluoresces a blue tinge, uranium, which is yellow but has a green surface tinge, pale pink eosin (made from diluting red ink) fluoresces orange, and a crimson solution of Magdala-red gives out scarlet.

May I again stress the fact that glass is practically opaque to ultra-violet light, although quartz can be used satisfactorily. Coloured glass also helps from a point of view of conducting experiments : red glass, for instance, cuts out all the rays of visible light except red, but glass coloured a deep violet with manganese and cobalt transmits a fair proportion of the ultra-violet part of the spectrum mixed with naturally visible violet. Using quinine as a fluorescent substance the part of the spectrum beyond the violet can be seen as being of a lavender colour.

By breaking up white light by means of a quartz prism and collecting through a biconvex lens made of very thin glass containing a solution of dicyanin in alcohol, a band of pale lavender colour can be brought into focus beyond the violet. The rays responsible for this extra colour are presumably ultra-violet rays.

Phosphorescence depends to some extent upon temperature. Professor Dewar showed that many substances became phosphorescent at a temperature of 200° below zero—substances that exhibit no tendency whatever to possess this property at normal temperatures—for example, feathers, paper and ivory.

Substances appear to store luminescence when very cold and to emit it when they are warmed, though on allowing them to cool down again the property is found no longer to exist on re-warming. Thus this storing of luminescence requires intense cold, while warming causes them to give up all their store.

Before closing this chapter on the preparation of screens, and apparatus in general, I may mention the evolution of my own screen.

I decided that dicyanin, as the best substance discovered at the time, must be persevered with.

Since this is insoluble in water it is made into an alcoholic solution. This evaporates very readily so must be contained in an absolutely air-tight screen.

Again, since sunlight causes the dye to deteriorate, it must be kept in the dark when not in use.

My first screens were thin sheets of glass cemented very close together—in fact, minute glass tanks. Principal difficulties : (1) Getting them made in England where even the most elementary type of glass cement appears to be unknown. (2) The quantity of dye solution required to fill them. From these evolved the hollow lenses.

It is naturally important to see that no other light reaches the eye except that which is passing through the screen. I used to cover my head with a cloth like photographers do. Actually I found my 'Varsity degree hood just the thing. Later, I set up the lenses in the collapsible goggles, the part between the lenses and the eyes, at the sides, being of a black material. Lining with fur around the eyes makes the cups light-proof, though personally I find it has the disadvantage of causing the brows to sweat. Any form of moisture on the lenses, of course, completely blots out the aura both by making the screen less transparent and also by refracting the rays. Moisture in the atmosphere is *one* of the reasons why ultra-violet rays are lost on entering our atmosphere, causing only a small percentage to reach us.

I am at present experimenting with hollow lenses that will contain the dye in solution of the best strength, though this will vary slightly with different eyes. I hope to cement it into the lenses to prevent evaporation. The trouble is that in time the dye will deteriorate, and so the lens will need refilling. I have, I think, hit upon a dye very like dicyanin, which is a better sensitizer and which will deteriorate only very slowly. I intend to put these more or less perfected screens upon the market. Many people have wanted screens for their own use and have found even dicyanin both difficult to obtain and expensive. If bought in larger quantities I believe screens could be produced that would cover the cost of production. My original screen cost me about ten pounds ! I can fix up an individual screen now for about three pounds. Two lenses mounted in collapsible goggles filled with dye solution. It should be possible to reduce the cost considerably by making a quantity. Having tried everywhere, I find that hollow lenses have to be got from Germany where they are produced excellently, of good quality glass—not quartz, of course, that would be prohibitive—and either plane, plano-convex, double convex or what you will. Personally, I have been fortunate in getting these for ten shillings each lens, with duty on top of this again. This sounds expensive, as it undoubtedly is, but it took me a long time and much trouble to obtain even these, although I had the help of a friend who had extensive business connexions with a glass apparatus firm in Germany as well as over here.

It seemed to me that a couple of watch glasses ought to be able to be stuck together for a few shillings, the glasses thrown in. Try ! I am always grateful for advice ; I naturally have to wait weeks for my lenses—and for my dye.

Purple glass will have the same effect at first sight. Everything looks reddy mauve or bluey mauve. I tried getting an exact match in colour with my dye, thinking that by this means some help might be obtained for beginners cheaply. These do not sensitize the retina and, although the foliage, flowers, etc., when viewed through them, look much as they look through the real screen, the ability to appreciate ultra-violet rays will not be acquired. Try looking at, say, yellows with the sun upon them. A dandelion through the purple glass looks mauve ; through the dye it will appear a flaming cerise. The latter seems to give the foliage life, the former merely makes everything dead mauve, shades between light and dark purple—instead of blues *and* reds.

A cheaper dye which would not deteriorate if exposed to the air directly so that it would be possible to paint a glass with it, would be a boon indeed. The chief trouble lies in making the hollow lens and keeping the solution from evaporating out of it.

I have said earlier that it is a moot point as to whether the effect on the eye is due entirely to the dye, or whether the colour really plays a part simply because it is of a particular colour. Dicyanin that is not just the right colour sensitizes but slowly. The purple glasses alone are quite useless.

The dye, of course, is the essential. It is solely responsible for sensitization. The colour possibly helps to cut out certain rays which tend to prevent sensitization or slow it down.

Dicyanin works slowly in comparison with my pinacyanol mixture. Dicyanin is more blue, less purple. There is more than one kind of pinacyanol ; one kind that I have had is only sparingly soluble in alcohol—and absolute alcohol at that, though it can be made to dissolve in one of the other alcohols.

Probably the aura when first seen will appear as a lighter purple vapour around the darker purple skin.

Later, the differentiation between the component parts of the aura will be picked out. Peculiarities in the aura, such as colour—blues and greys—will not come at once. When the whole of the aura can be seen it is by no means easy to keep it in view at first. Most people see *something* without, of course, being able to differentiate between the inside and the outer parts. The inside aura usually is the first part to be identified definitely, which means in all probability that something has appeared, perhaps subconsciously, beyond it, for it seems to have a distinct straight distal margin. Then the outer haze appears extending considerably beyond the first part. It will be seen stretching out beyond the tips of the fingers. To me it appears rather like a *mist*, never quite still, yet one could not say how or in what direction it moved. By comparison, I might liken the inside aura to water, still, shallow water, and yet when it becomes clearer it is certainly striped.

It is the misty haze that offers most difficulty, just as it also offers greater possibilities. Things worth having usually are more difficult to acquire—and here is perhaps the chief difficulty, the one I have mentioned, that of keeping it in view when you have discovered it. It must be viewed not by staring directly *at* it. It is being registered on the rods of the retina, not on the fovea centralis, and therefore one has to look to the side of it, *just* to the side of it—by no means an easy thing to do without practice. There seems to be a temptation to gaze at it as it were to try to get it into better focus, for it is faint, not very obvious, especially when one first discovers it. This must be persevered with ; practice makes it easier to see without looking directly at the haze, and also the cumulative effect of the dye tends to make the eye more sensitive to these rays and so makes them more easily distinguished.

CHAPTER IV

IS THE INSIDE AURA OUR ELECTRIC FIELD?

WE now reach the much more difficult question as to whether the
aura contains, or does not contain,
electrically charged particles. It has already
been pointed out that the outer haze, at least,
is made up of ultra-violet rays. These, of course,
will not be material—that is to say, they will contain no solid substance. The rays from the sun
pass through space. They do not warm the space
because there is no solid matter there to be
warmed. When heat is radiated from a hot
body, the heat rays impart heat to all and sundry
colder bodies which lie in their path. Much the
same thing may be said to apply to rays of light—
and also to the shorter waves of ultra-violet
" light."

These rays, I suggest, are radiated from the
living body and, by the means already described, it is possible to see them. Of such,
in fact, is the outer haze of our aura—rays,
containing no solid matter. The inside aura,

though, it was suggested, you will remember, displayed magnetic attraction.

This fact alone can be explained in one way only, viz. that it must contain some solid particles, for magnets cannot affect rays of light.

No magnet, let me repeat, either electric or horse-shoe or bar magnet, exerts any pull upon the outer haze. It is only the inside aura that is suspected of containing solid particles.

First of all, faintness causes the aura, all of it, to fade—and later to return gradually. Very contradictory, all this, at first sight.

If we agree that the aura can be emitted only by a *living* body, we can readily understand that loss of consciousness might, in fact *should*, cause this to happen. Return of consciousness would then very naturally cause the body again to emit its aura, both the inside one containing solid particles and the rays of ultra-violet wave-length which give rise to the haze beyond.

Again, when the subject undergoing inspection was given an electric charge by means of a Wimshurst machine, the aura, the inside part only, was found to fade—and later to return somewhat expanded.

The outer haze was practically unaffected, though it appeared to be slightly dimmed, possibly only by comparison, particularly at its distal edge.

Let us consider the facts carefully and see whether we can account for them satisfactorily.

The charge, whether similar or dissimilar, causes the inside aura to vanish, and then to settle down expanded. Nothing unusual here, surely. The expanded aura is no doubt the inside aura with its electrically charged particles encroaching upon the outer haze. The differentiation between the two auras is certainly less marked. The very slight fading in brightness of the outer haze, if it is not purely imaginary, must be put down to the effect of some slight shock due to the charge, bringing about a condition similar in a very minor degree to that produced by death or in the case of faintness. *I have ventured to suggest that this haze is of ectodermal origin and should, therefore, be affected by anything that the nervous system registers.*

Solids either are attracted by magnets, in which case they are said to be magnetic ; or they are not affected, in which case they are said to be non-magnetic. Certain metals exhibit this magnetic property, namely iron, nickel and cobalt. The particles in the case of the aura would undoubtedly be iron.

Magnetic substances must now be subdivided into " magnetic " : those which are attracted to a magnet, no matter which end of the magnet is presented, and " actual magnets." Magnets attract other magnets, but they will also repel them. Suppose we suspend by a piece of cotton a small magnet, it will set with its north seeking pole turned towards the magnetic north, as in the case of a compass. The other end of the magnet, the south seeking pole, will be repelled by the earth's north pole, and so will turn towards the south.

If the particles contained in our aura were actual magnets, they should run to a magnet, it is true, but if the magnet were to be turned round so that the other end of it were presented to the particles, the aura should then draw away. As I have stated, many people believe that this does happen, thus accounting very neatly for instinctive likes and dislikes. Personally I have not found that a magnet will repel the inside aura, and, therefore, I must consider its particles to be merely magnetic, but not actual magnets.

Cases have been quoted of magnets being brought into close proximity with the body, presumably into the field of the inside aura, with the result that the subject felt actual physical pain. One case in particular is vouched for by a very creditable witness who testified that, during the progress of a particularly violent thunderstorm, he found that a woman subject screamed out in pain when a bar magnet was brought near her. A little later the magnet was again brought up to her body, without her knowledge this time, when the result was just the same. She became conscious of its presence instantly and located its exact position, somewhere on the back where she could not possibly have seen the magnet.

Next let me compare certain conditions brought about by the body when it has been subjected to a charge of electricity with those exhibited by the inside aura : It must be remembered that, when the body is charged with electricity by a Wimshurst machine, the electric charge will extend over the skin, that is to say, it will be purely a surface charge.

In the case of the natural aura I am suggesting, though it is only fair for me to point out that others do not agree with me here, that this part of the aura is of endodermal origin, and, therefore, comes from some way *beneath* the skin, in which case its charge must penetrate the skin so as to form an electric field of influence around it, viz. the inside aura.

In the case of the charge upon the skin, friction sometimes increases the charge. This is not the case where the aura is concerned. Massaging the skin does not alter the aura's appearance appreciably.

Damping the skin also has no effect upon the aura.

Charged conductors have a much wider field around points than around flat surfaces. The aura, too, extends further from the points of the fingers than it does in the neighbourhood of the palms of the hands, for instance. The same may be noticed in respect of the elbow, when the hands are placed on the hips, as opposed to the forearm or upper arm. In the latter instance the *inside* aura extends perhaps only half an inch, whereas around the trunk it will extend much further, not because the trunk is angular or pointed, but just because it is much bigger. When the hands are placed upon the hips the outer haze from the trunk will overlap that from the arm. The haze will here appear brighter than elsewhere. Always ask your subject to place her hands on her hips when you are inspecting the outer haze. You will be able to distinguish its colour more easily here.

The aura around the head is often wide, but the width is due almost entirely to extended outer haze—actually the inside aura is very narrow, extending but little beyond the hair in a man, and being completely hidden by a woman's tresses. What does this suggest? Let us see : Reverting once again to our " earthworm " days, it will be found that there is no brain in such animals. The worm's body consists, as I have already pointed out, of a skin (ectoderm) and a digestive tract (endoderm) ; in between these two cylinders, in the mesoderm, lies, among other things, the nerve cord. This runs from end to end of the worm ventrally. At the anterior end the nerve cord terminates in a pair of ganglia.

Going a little higher up the ladder of Evolution we come to the molluscs and the arthropods, where we find slightly better developed " brain " ganglia. Mounting higher still we arrive at the vertebrates. First the fish ; then the amphibians, represented in England to-day by the frog, the toad and the newt, and next the reptiles. These were much bigger than the present-day ones, but their brain, though showing a steady improvement upon the invertebrate animals, was much inferior to that of their successors, the mammals. And so the intellect increases from the days of the earliest mammals who probably looked something like the South African dassies—not unlike guinea-pigs—and who conquered the monstrous reptiles by the simple device of eating their eggs, through the various intermediate stages, none of which exists to-day (for all have progressed, some more rapidly than others, but not along a common path), till we come to the cat type, the bush baby (the Moholi Lemur of to-day), the ring-tailed monkey, the apes and so to *Homo sapiens*, as Man is modestly called.

From this we see how the brain has developed out of the swollen end of the nerve cord. *The nervous system originates from the ectoderm. The ectoderm and the mesoderm are, I suggest, responsible for the outer haze.*

The outer haze is wide in the neighbourhood of the spine also, wide certainly by comparison with the inside aura—of course, the spinal column of the vertebrate corresponds to the ventral nerve in the earthworm and the lobster, the spinal cord in the higher animals running in a backbone instead of being situated ventrally. There is, however, a well-marked inside aura, possibly affected favourably by the notochord.

I do not pretend to state that the electricity is given off by the endoderm, of course ; presumably the auras from the ectoderm, mesoderm and endoderm will overlap one another, gradually blending the one into the other. I do say, though, that the differentiation, as represented by the visible margin between the two parts of the aura, is due to the fact that the ultra-violet rays extend beyond the electrically charged particles which intermingle with that part of the aura emitted as the inside aura.

Even this statement must not be taken as fact by any manner of means. Much more research must be carried out, and will, I trust, be carried out by men of science far abler than I.

The theory that the outer haze originates from the mesoderm and the ectoderm, while certain facts point to the possibility of the endoderm's being responsible for the inside aura, is a theory of mine merely—and I offer it as food for reflection.

I feel much more sure regarding the outer haze than I do about the inside aura, concerning which there is certainly one obstacle at least to be overcome, namely, observations where muscles have received damage. The muscles are not of endodermal origin, and yet the damaged part, it seems, emits no inside aura, or practically none.

It can be shown by means of a galvanometer

that a trace of a current exists from the end of a muscle to the middle, i.e. with an external circuit from middle to ends. This current used to be known as the natural muscle current.

It has since been shown by Hermann that this is not true of a resting muscle, but that the current is due to the injury caused in preparation, and that the current varies directly with the extent of the injury. To quote Hermann : " In partially injured muscles every point of the injured part is negative towards the points of the uninjured surface."

Starling tells us that when a muscle is quite dead this current of rest ceases, the current being due to electrical difference between the living and the dying, though not dead, tissue.

Whatever may be the explanation of this current in the resting muscle, there is certainly an electrical charge when a muscle contracts. Whether this electrical presence registers its effect upon the inside aura, I do not know with any degree of certainty ; injured muscles do quite definitely bring about an alteration in the appearance of this part of the aura. I am not suggesting that this electricity is responsible for the inside aura, far from it. There is much more evidence in favour of its having its origin in the endoderm.

Let us now consider just what we mean by " endoderm." We need not go back as far as the worm again for this ; we will consider the development of the egg of Amphioxus, the lancelet. The development of this lowest type of vertebrate in some ways resembles that of a mammal.

The fertilized ovum is a single microscopic cell. The first division is a longitudinal one ; so is the second, at right angles to the first. The third is equatorial, dividing the ovum into an upper animal pole consisting of four cells and a vegetative pole also of four cells below it.

Next come two longitudinal planes of segmentation, followed by two equatorial ones. Thus segmentation continues until 256 cells are formed, when a hollow sphere, called the blastosphere, results.

Now follows gastrulation. Imagine a tennis ball painted half blue, the animal pole, and half red, the vegetative pole. Place your thumbs together in the middle of the red and by pressure turn this half inwards until it lies immediately under the blue. Then suppose the edges of the blue are drawn over to meet. We now have a half ball (gastrula=a cup) blue on the outside and red on the inside.

This red is, roughly speaking, the hypoblast, or endoderm. The blue part will be the epiblast or ectoderm.

The epiblast flattens on the future dorsal side forming the future nerve cord.

The mesoblast forms between the epiblast and the primitive hypoblast. Thus we have the three germinal layers. The hypoblast produces the lining of the alimentary canal and the glands that open into it, also the notochord.

The mesoblast is responsible for the reproductive and excretory organs, the blood vessels, the muscles and connective tissue, while the skin and the nervous system come from the epiblast, as I have mentioned previously.

Although part of the inside aura is material, I am by no means satisfied that all of it is. It is probable that it may contain some rays emitted by the endoderm in addition to those forming the outer haze which will, as I have suggested, run through the " country " allotted to the inside aura *en route* for their own beyond. That the inside aura contains *some* solid matter is, I maintain, beyond dispute— the magnets have shown this.

Now let us turn to some of the evidence in favour of its endoderm origin :

A case of a woman who had suffered for some years from chronic indigestion had a faint inside aura, particularly over the stomach area, yet the outer haze was good. Later, she became nervous and depressed, when her outer haze showed a bulge in the neighbourhood of the spine when viewed from the side. This bulge was not very much pronounced, presumably because the nerviness was not of long standing.

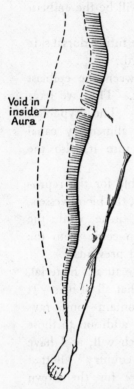

Void in inside Aura

No inside aura emitted over area where appendix had just been removed.

Another case, where a subject had recently had his vermiform appendix removed, offers confirmatory evidence. The outer haze was clear and, for a man, wide. The inside aura was of average brightness, but there was a dull streak over the appendix area—so narrow that it appeared like a black ray —rather a contradictory explanation, but descriptive, for the strip was not an inch wide. It was due undoubtedly to the fact that there was *no* aura emitted there. It represented, in fact, a void, no aura being present just at the place where its source had been removed.

One wonders why other parts of the intestine in the neighbourhood did not supply an aura. I can only repeat that the void was very narrow.

Yet another man who told me that he had recently had an operation upon his liver, though was not very clear as to the exact nature, when examined, his inside aura in the neighbourhood of the liver, on one side more than on the other, was very weak indeed, while the haze beyond was normal.

Incidentally a case of a floating kidney—the kidney was very movable and gave a good deal of pain—the inside aura, when viewed from the side, was weak in the small of the back, while the outer haze was wide and bow-shaped. This case supplies much conflicting evidence—one would have expected the outer haze alone to have been affected. The subject was neurotic ; hence the bowed haze—this is as it should be— but the floating kidney made no marked impression upon the outer haze, while it seemed to have affected the inside aura. This might perhaps be accounted for, though, by the fact that the injury was due to the subject's being thrown from a horse out hunting and dragged. Much bruising must have been caused to the muscles and possibly other injuries were sustained, the nature of which was not disclosed.

Bruising of muscles often causes a striation of the inside aura, the texture of which is noticeably different over the points of injury than elsewhere.

Ultra-violet rays possess the power of nullifying the charge upon an electrified surface. This has been known for a long time. Professor Hertz found that surfaces carrying an electric charge, such as the leaves of a gold leaf electroscope, could be diselectrified by ultraviolet rays. If, however, the electrified surface is metal surrounded by air the ultra-violet rays falling upon it will bring about diselectrification only if the surface carries a negative charge. Professor Thompson found, though, that a surface of lead peroxide if surrounded by hydrogen can be diselectrified by these rays if the electrification is positive.

This suggests that the different kinds of lightwaves have different photo-electric as well as different photo-chemical powers.

There are many points to be cleared up before one can locate all the sources that appear to affect the inside aura, and many more subjects for inspection than are likely to come my way will be necessary to supply a width of experience which alone can settle the points at issue.

Now, I have said that massage does not materially affect the aura. I mean, of course, that by the friction more surface electricity does not appear to be produced. I have already expressed my belief that this inside aura is of endodermal origin and therefore comes from beneath the skin upon which the friction is being applied. Neither does wetting the skin alter the width or intensity of this more material emission. This is, however, possible—it is in fact practicable—namely, that a body may be able to impart a slight, though none the less beneficial, current to another body whose potential is lower. I know of one medical practitioner who makes use of this in massage. I myself have been treated by him for rheumatism with some success. The principle is obvious enough. If we emit electrically charged particles we must contain a certain amount of electricity—we must contain charge. Since some people have a more intense inside aura than others, i.e. a stronger field, it follows that not every body is charged to the same potential. If two bodies are at different potentials and they come into contact, a current of electricity will flow from the body at the higher potential to the one at the lower. If the skin be covered with water this should tend to help the passage of this current. My skin was damped with something in a bottle, and this doctor placed his fingers over the painful shoulder-joint. He made but little attempt to rub. I soon felt a pleasing glow passing through my shoulder. I admitted being mildly surprised at so obvious a result for so little apparent action. I tumbled to what was happening and asked whether the liquid with which my shoulder had been rubbed were not water—for I could think of no more suitable liquid for the purpose. The doctor smiled, and explained just what his principle was. My rheumatism had been acquired some ten or twelve years earlier than this, presumably by exposure, and since it has yielded to no treatment he had felt justified in trying the effect of his state of higher potential—call it radiant health, if you will—upon me. The effect naturally was not lasting, though I believe that had I been able to continue the treatment I should have received benefit until my potential had been raised more nearly to that of the doctor who told me that he had to keep himself in perfect condition to enable him to impart electricity to others. He felt no ill effects as a result of doing so, for the drop in potential at each sitting would be infinitesimal. A hyper-fit man should be able to impart a beneficial current, which is not a strong current, to a man who is run down—call it a healing touch, that is what it might easily amount to in an extreme case. Surely a miracle becomes no less worthy of belief because a simple, well-known and " every day " phenomenon has been made use of for its performance; rather does it become more easy of belief? Christ probably had this high potential and used it as an agent through which some of His miracles were performed.

Though there are other recognized explanations, I think this may be one of the reasons for His asking Mary not to touch Him when she met Him in the Garden after the Resurrection. Had she done so, possibly the result might have been fatal to her.

This living electricity, if one may so describe it, is far more beneficial than that generated by an inanimate object can ever be. The aura of such a highly charged individual would be of remarkable intensity. I cannot pick up rays from an arc lamp with my screen to anything like sufficient a degree to consider them in the light of being an aura. Clearly something more than mere ultra-violet rays, or machine-made electricity, is emitted by the living body in the form of what I refer to as an aura. Just what the difference is remains to be proved.

CHAPTER V

A VERY brief description of the structure and functions of the human eye may not be entirely out of place before going into the subject further. I intend to set this out more or less in the form of notes, aided by a diagram rather than entering into a lengthy discussion. Text books on Optics or on elementary Biology already contain very able descriptions upon which I certainly cannot improve. This, however, may act as a memory refresher and may help to clarify much of my later discussions.

Sclerotic Coat : Tough, white outer covering to which muscles are attached for pulling eyeball. Modified in front into transparent *cornea*, a dust-proof covering washed by secretion from the infra-orbital gland, and shielded by the eyelids, the pink fleshy structure in the mesial corner being a remnant of the nictitating membrane, or third eyelid, so often seen covering the eyes of birds.

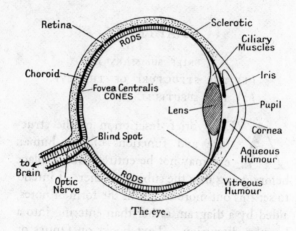

The eye.

Choroid coat : Dark lining to sclerotic. Contains blood-vessels for nourishment. Modified in front into muscles :

1. *Iris*, which regulates the size of the aperture (pupil) which varies inversely as the strength of the light.
2. *Ciliary Muscles*, which pull on the back of the lens so as to alter its convexity. It thus will be enabled to bring into focus upon the retina images of both near and distant objects. This power is known as *accommodation*, the lack of which power

results in long or short sight, and is corrected by the addition of glasses with convex or concave lenses respectively.

Retina : Inner lining sensitized by Optic Nerve which carries impulses of sight from retina to brain. Consists of nerve-endings :

1. *Cones :* most plentiful in *fovea centralis*. Functions : clear vision and colour.
2. *Rods :* most plentiful in periphery. Function only in dim light when all objects appear blue-grey.

The cones and rods have been dealt with fully in another chapter, so there is no need to discuss them further here.

Yellow Spot (macula lutea) : Part of retina immediately opposite to pupil. Diameter *circa* 2 mm. The centre of the yellow spot is the *fovea centralis*.

Blind Spot : Place where Optic Nerve enters retina. Usually about 1¼ mm. on the nasal side of the macula lutea. Not sensitive to light. Its existence can easily be demonstrated by making a dot and a cross about six inches apart upon a piece of paper which is held horizontally with the cross on the right of the dot.

If the left eye is closed and one gazes at the dot, the cross can be seen out of the corner of the right eye when the paper is held at arm's length.

As it is brought closer the cross will be found to disappear when the blind spot is reached, but upon bringing the paper nearer still—or by turning it out of the horizontal—the cross will reappear. Much has been written about the blind spot, however, by cricket coaches in favour of, or against, the two-eyed stance; there can be no useful purpose served by my dwelling further upon its existence here.

Aqueous Humour : A liquid substance between the cornea and the lens, and

Vitreous Humour : A jelly-like substance behind the lens—these keep the eye from collapsing. Both have about the same refractive index.

Let us consider for a moment the various media through which rays have to pass on entering the eye before they can reach the retina. All these media are capable of refracting the rays, and also of bringing the different colours to focus at different places, to the almost exclusion of anything with shorter wave-length than that of violet light.

As regards the different focus of colours,

chromatic aberration does not take place to any marked degree on the passage of light through the lens (which is a kind of many-sided prism) as the light is white light. A bundle of red rays and a parallel bundle of blue rays each striking the lens parallel to the principal axis would meet the axis produced behind the lens at different points, the blue in front of the red.

With white light this must happen in the same way, though we are not aware of it. The brain has become accustomed to it. I have said in an earlier chapter that probably the yellows are focused exactly on the retina with the blues a trifle short and the reds behind it. The focal length of the lens thus differs for rays of different colours, but the difference is very slight indeed. The focus of the lens is about 43·7 mm. Refraction due to media, i.e. making the image appear closer than it really is—just as a coin placed under a slab of glass appears to be raised up above the surface of the table—is easily overcome by the brain's accustoming itself to receiving impulses of objects through refracted media. After all, the images received through the lens of the eye are inverted ones. The brain causes them to appear erect. We acquire functions for our various parts to suit our surroundings.

Here are the media passed through : cornea, aqueous humour, lens and vitreous humour. The rays may be refracted at these surfaces : front and back surfaces of cornea, and front and back surfaces of lens.

The refractive indices of the cornea, the aqueous and the vitreous humours, are almost identical : 1·336. They may, therefore, be treated as though they were one substance. Let us call them " eye substance." The refractive index of the lens is 1·437. We now have virtually only two media, viz. the " eye substance " and the lens. The refractive surfaces that will matter thus will be reduced to three. The front of the cornea and the front and the back of the lens.

The obstacles to be cleared by the rays may be stated as follows :

(*a*) Radius of curvature of cornea, 8 mm.

(*b*) Thickness of cornea+aqueous humour, 3·6 mm.

(*c*) Radius of curvature of front of lens, 10 mm.

(*d*) Thickness of lens, about 3·6 mm.

(*e*) Radius of curvature of back of lens, 6 mm. [This will vary. " Accommodation."]

(*f*) Thickness of vitreous humour.

Tables show that the focal distance of the front of the cornea is 23 mm. while that of the lens is 44 mm.

The reciprocals of these numbers added together give us the reciprocal of the joint focal distance, i.e. that of the whole eye, 15 mm. Clearly the front surface of the cornea is of first importance.

The short-sighted eye cannot see distant objects clearly, since the power of accommodation does not allow the ciliary muscles to pull the lens sufficiently to make it bring the rays into focus exactly on the retina.

Long sight— also old sight—is caused by the lens's being pulled too much to bring near objects into clear focus.

In my introduction I have mentioned briefly how

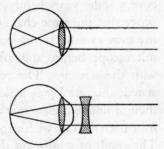

Short sight corrected by concave lens.

I first came to discover that the dye used tended to correct long sight. Kilner found that he had to readjust the focus of his microscope after using the dye. He was, however, years older than I am. Good though his eyes must have been, even the very best eyes will lose their power of accommodation as we age.

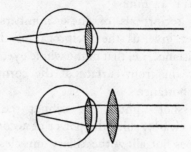

Long sight corrected by convex lens.

Finding that Kilner had also made this discovery some years before, I at once set out to prove that the same change had taken place in my own eyes by trying out their focus on my microscope before and after sensitizing them with the screens. The result was, as already stated, the one I was looking and hoping for, though not to such a marked degree as would have been the case with an older man, obviously. The result of sensitizing the eyes, therefore, is the equivalent to the wearing of a convex lens, but without the danger which from a point of view of playing games is pretty considerable. The effect is, however, temporary. No lasting harm, or good, will come to the eyes through using the screens.

The dye that I use is not the same as that used by Kilner, though possibly his dicyanin may suit some eyes as well as my sensitizer. That each individual must answer for him- or herself. Ultra-violet rays made artificially by a quartz mercury arc will affect certain tissue in a hen's egg. After one hour egg albumen will have coagulated. There will be no appreciable coagulation of the albuminous tissue of the eye, such as the humours, after a week. The egg white is coagulated by ultra-violet rays below the stimulative region, from as long as $310 \ \mu\mu$ to 265, this latter wave-length having the more marked effect. The presence of certain salts, the chlorides of magnesium and calcium, and sodium silicate, though too weak to affect the transparency of the lens, will, if subjected to ultra-violet rays in this region, produce opacity resulting possibly in cataract. These same salts when applied to the skin will tend to hasten sunburn if ultra-violet rays are present, not otherwise ; the rays in this case may be of even longer wave-length, such as those of the solar ultra-violet region, the aura country. Back along, folks used to sun-bathe sores on their skins, believing that they were cured. Quite sound ; the shorter of the sun's ultra-violet rays would kill the germs. Minute creatures do not like ultra-short rays, as can be seen by watching the effect of sunshine upon the small inhabitants of sea water.

Blue rays penetrate the water to a depth of about 500 metres, while ultra-violet ones will reach twice that distance. No radiation can probe beyond 1700 metres. Rays necessary for vegetation do not extend beyond 600 metres. The fact that the presence of bacteria and of plankton is increased in winter suggests that even the solar ultra-violet rays act as sterilizers. Plankton is rarer in the sunny seas than in those of foggy areas.

Further experiments dealing with the effect of the longer ultra-violet rays upon animals will be given in a chapter dealing with the aura and its possible appearance to eyes other than our own.

It must be remembered that the wave-length of a ray varies inversely as its frequency. There are rays whose wave-lengths are too great to stimulate vision. There are also rays whose refractive index is such that they can never reach the retina. The visible spectrum is only a small patch in the complete spectrum. There are also patches that have not been very fully explored, one between the infra-red country and the wireless waves which are

TABLE

THE VISIBLE SPECTRUM AND THE ULTRA-VIOLET COUNTRY

[1 millimicron, $\mu\mu$, = 10 angstrom units = 1 millionth of 1 mm.]

$\lambda = \mu\mu.$

30,000–800	Heat	
800–650	Red	
650–600	Orange	The colours of the visible spectrum. There are, however, no hard and fast lines as the colours gradually merge the one into the other.
600–560	Yellow	
560–530	Green	
530–490	Blue	
490–450	Indigo	
450–400	Violet	

400–340 Long wave ultra-violet. Harmless to the eyes. Emitted by electric arc with carbon poles. Transmitted by thin glass.

340–300 Harmless to the eyes. Emitted by uviol mercury lamp. Transmitted by Jena crown glass.

Present in white light. Stimulative.

300–220 Emitted by quartz mercury arc lamp. Transmitted by fused quartz.

220–180 Transmitted by thickish layers of crystalline quartz or rocksalt.

180–140 Transmitted possibly by fluorspar. Absorbed by air.

Germicidal.

50– 01 X-rays.

·01–0 Gamma rays.

The aura rays are presumably 400–300 $\mu\mu$.

electro-magnetic, and another between our own hunting ground, the ultra-violet, and the much shorter X-rays.

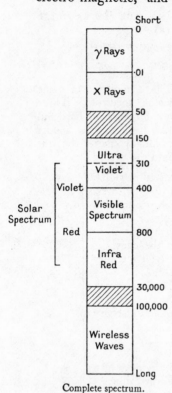

Complete spectrum.

The figures in the right-hand margin give the corresponding wave-lengths expressed in millionths of a millimetre.

X-rays were first discovered by Röntgen. He covered a tube completely with black paper and passed an electric discharge through it; a fluorescent screen placed a few yards away was made to shine brightly, and objects placed between the screen and the tube cast shadows. The radiation coming from the tube thus could not be ultra-violet "light," since it was able to pass through the black paper. X-rays appeared to be neither reflected nor refracted, but it has since been shown that they differ from ordinary visible light only in respect of the

88

length of their waves. Sound waves will echo off a brick wall, but the surface of the wall is too uneven to reflect light. This is the reason why X-rays cannot be reflected. Even the recognized reflecting surfaces such as mirrors are not sufficiently smooth for the purpose.

A mirror will reflect the comparatively large waves of visible light, but the very act of polishing causes roughness too great to allow reflexion of the minute X-ray waves whose length is *circa* one five-thousandth of that of visible light. Rutherford's gamma rays emitted by Mme Curie's element, radium, are even shorter still. They have tremendous power of penetration and are deflected neither by magnets nor by electricity. The electro-magnetic wireless waves, the X-rays and the gamma rays, though differing widely in properties, are fundamentally different only in wave-length.

To sum up :

Alpha rays

1. Are given off by all radio-active substances.

2. Are deflected to a comparatively small extent in a magnetic field.

3. Have a limited power of penetration, being absorbed by even a thin layer of matter.

4. Have great power to ionize a gas, making it a conductor.

5. Have but little effect upon a photographic plate.

6. Produce phosphorescence in sulphide of zinc.

7. Are large. An α ion has a mass of *circa* twice that of a hydrogen ion—and are perhaps discharged helium atoms.

8. α ions carry a positive charge.

9. Have a velocity about one-tenth of that of light, which is 186,000 miles per second.

Beta rays

1. Are given off by nearly all radio-active substances.

2. Are very easily deflected in a magnetic field.

3. Are absorbed by matter, but less so than α rays are.

4. Comparatively small power to ionize a gas.

5. Can cause the production of phosphorescence, but less so than in the case of α rays.

6. Effect on photographic plate, poor.

7. Mass *circa* one-seven hundred and seventieth of a hydrogen ion.

8. Carry a negative charge.

9. Velocity the same as that of light.

Apart from velocity, are very similar to cathode ray in tube.

Gamma rays.

1. Exist wherever β rays exist.

2. Have tremendous powers of penetration.

3. Much less power to ionize a gas.

4. Are not affected by magnets.

5. Considerable effect upon photographic plate.

6. Are able to produce phosphorescence.

7. Appear to be pulses set up in the ether by impact of β rays on solid matter.

All this is well known, I merely tabulate it for the convenience of my readers.

This brief discussion has but little to do with the aura, I know, but I trust it may help to give some idea of the relative position of the rays given off by the human body with regard to those of the rest of the complete spectrum.

CHAPTER VI

PHANTOM IMAGES AND VISUAL SENSATIONS

NO doubt everybody has tried forming phantom images, such as staring at a coloured picture of a Union Jack for a few moments and then transferring the gaze to a piece of white paper. The phantom image of the flag will appear on the paper, though, as it fades, the colours will in all probability change.

This power of carrying a phantom image of an object to another background requires one essential—a background. The image cannot be reformed in mid-air.

I intend to show that these phantom colours can be carried from a coloured object and reformed on the aura. Such phantoms will appear a little in front of and at the sides of the body. What is the background on which they are being formed ? Obviously it can be nothing else than the aura.

I have found, though, that such images do

not appear upon the outer haze, but only on the inside aura, which confirms, to some extent, my contention that the outer haze is not material, being composed of rays of ultra-violet wave-length, while the inside aura may be substantial, at least in part, perhaps containing particles carrying an electric charge.

The colour of the aura is, I contend, always some shade of blue or grey. Let me make it quite clear that these phantom colours are, of course, entirely *subjective* ; they are optical illusions, so to speak, being formed on the retina and transferred to another place, in this case, to the aura, as an image on the retina—an image which gradually fades. The colour seen is not formed by the aura which is playing no part in the formation other than by acting as a solid background.

Let us now consider the eye itself. The minute endings of sensory neurones lie massed together in the sensitive layer of the retina. When rays of light fall on these certain chemical changes take place.

Some of these neurones are known as *cones* and are responsible for clear vision and for the interpretation of colour. Others are called *rods* ; these function at night or in a dim light only.

Let us study the cones first :

These are situated in the centre of the retina, that part on which the image is formed when the object is looked at directly. They function in

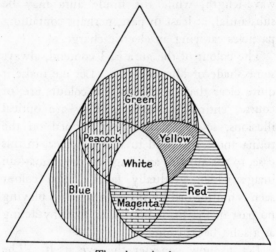

The colour triangle.

bright light, artificial as well as daylight, but not at night.

Some of these neurones are red-sensitive, some yellow- or green-sensitive and some blue sensitive. The other colours are produced by a mixture of any *two* kinds in varying proportions—e.g. suppose at a particular point the green and the blue are functioning, then the

94

colours seen would be the blue-greens. Now suppose that the red-sensitive neurones are gradually brought into play, the blue-green shade will not change to orange, it will become a paler blue-green—until the full quota of red neurones become active, when white light will result.

In short : there are only three elementary colours. The functioning of any two of these at the same spot on the retina causes the intermediate shades to be seen, but all three working together produce white light.

Let us imagine spots of red, green and blue light being thrown upon a screen by three separate lamps. When the spots overlap the following results will be obtained :

Red + Green + Blue—> White
Red + Green—> Yellow ⎫ Complementary
Blue + Red—> Magenta ⎬ colours respec-
Green + Blue—> Peacock or ⎪ tively of Blue,
               Prussian Blue ⎭ Green and Red
Red + Prussian Blue—> White
Green + Magenta—> White
Blue + Yellow—> White
White dimmed becomes Grey

This is best demonstrated by arranging the colours in the form of a triangle as shown in the diagram; the three angles are represented by the three elementary colours, red, green and blue, these colours intermingling along the sides of the triangle, thus :

The red-green side will show yellow.

The green-blue side will show Prussian blue.

The red-blue side will show magenta.

The space in the middle of the triangle will be white.

From this it can be seen that when the elementary colour of any of the three angles mixes with the complementary colour of its opposite side, white light results. This is really what one would expect to happen, since the complementary colour in question contains the two elementary colours other than the one represented in its opposite angle. Thus we are using all three colours and, quite naturally, the result is white.

No doubt we can remember, as children, painting the rainbow colours on a disc of cardboard and spinning it round on a central pin in the form of a top. The flying rings of colour intermingled forming white—or, at least, grey.

Conversely, white light is split up into the colours of the spectrum on passing through a glass prism.

These neurones, then, the stimulation of which results in our appreciation respectively of the colours, red, green and blue, are situated in the centre of the retina, the fovea centralis.

I am not suggesting that every eye has the same number of neurones of each colour. The colour which I call canary, for instance, may appear to a person who has a preponderance of green-sensitive neurones as a greener yellow. This person will, of course, think of this greener yellow by the name of canary, as this is the name of the particular shade, as it has appeared to him, that he has always heard spoken of as canary.

Similarly the man who possesses more than his share of red-sensitive neurones will see a different shade again as canary. Thus, if the " green-sensitive " man could see his canary colour with the " red-sensitive " man's eyes, he would undoubtedly call it by quite another name.

Colours, therefore, may appear slightly different to each one of us. From this it can be understood that if only one set of these neurones were stimulated, say the blue-sensitive one, the eye would then see everything as blue.

On the other hand, let us suppose that one group, for instance the green, has become exhausted through extreme fatigue. The result would be temporary blindness to that colour and to resultant colours that contain it. The blue and the red will be functioning, so that all the colours that contain blue or red will be seen, though their respective shades will be somewhat modified owing to the absence of any green influence.

If two groups were temporarily to be put out of action at the same time, completely, not partially, of course, then monochromatic, or one colour, vision would result until the other two groups had recovered. Clearly this must be the case, since there would be no other colour to tone down either to a greater or a lesser degree the one remaining.

I have before me a coloured advertisement for somebody's mustard ; a mustard pot containing some very yellow mustard. I am gazing at the yellow mustard. This will have the effect of fatiguing the cone neurones of my retina, the stimulation of which neurones enables me to appreciate the colour yellow. Now I have transferred my gaze to a piece of white paper. The mustard pot appears, but the mustard is *blue*. Now the red neurones are turning the mustard from blue to purple—then to a paler shade, the colour of a not very ripe plum. Now the phantom has faded. Because the neurones (the stimulation of which is responsible for producing the colour yellow) were not being brought into play, no yellow colours could be seen at first, though they gradually exert their influence as the neurones recover.

Of course, if the conclusions drawn from experiments of this nature are to be of any value, the background on which the phantom is encouraged to appear must be a white one. A coloured background would tint the shades that are appearing in the phantom. May I again stress the fact that such phantoms and phantom colours are entirely subjective. They originate from the observer's own eyes and have nothing whatever to do with the object on which they are being formed, this object being nothing more than a background.

Before leaving the question of colour it is necessary, perhaps, to differentiate between coloured light and pigments. Mixtures of the three elementary colours make white light. Blue light plus yellow (which is a mixture of the other two elementary colours—green and red) make white light. Light is white before it is split up into its colours by a prism. Yet artists may say : " When we mix blue and yellow paint we get green, not white. Why is this ? "

Colours of pigments and of bodies in nature arise owing to the fact that most of the white light falling upon them penetrates for some distance, with the result that some of its constituent rays are absorbed before reflexion can take place. Thus it can be seen that yellow pigments appear that colour because, when white light falls upon them, blue and violet are absorbed, while green, yellow and red are reflected. Most yellows in nature are not pure, and reflect green and red as well as yellow. Blue pigments appear blue because they absorb yellow and red. Blues, too, as they occur in nature, are not always very pure, and they then reflect green in addition to blue. When blue and yellow pigments are mixed, therefore, the mixture absorbs all colours that are absorbed by either of its components—viz. blue, violet, yellow and red—the only colour left to be reflected remains green. Therefore, the mixture of blue and yellow *pigments* appears green. When a mixture is made of pigments one obtains only those colours which none of the components absorbs. This does not apply to the mixing of coloured *lights*.

There are still parts of the retina to be dealt with which are sensitized with neurones of a more elementary nature. These are the rods.

Possibly in earlier days eyes were sensitized entirely by rods before the cones were evolved. The rods are situated further from the centre of the retina, so that they are not brought into play by absolutely direct vision. The boundary between the cones and the rods is not a hard and fast one ; there is a zone where a mixture of the two kinds of neurones is to be found. The peripheral region consists almost entirely of rods. As this region is approached the proportion of cones not only decreases, but the actual cones become more rod-like in structure. The rods function at night or in a light too dim to cause stimulation of the cones.

One cannot recognize colours with the rods. When they only are being used everything looks *greyish blue*.

Rays of normally visible wave-length all look greyish blue, whatever colour they would appear to the cones—*all except red*. Red rays, and rays of longer wave-length than that producing red, have no effect upon the rods.

I believe that the rods, in an appropriate light, are capable of receiving rays, the wave-length of which is slightly shorter than that producing violet, and of translating them into visible light.

Grey-blue *objects* seen by the rods must not

be confused in any way with phantom *images*. There is nothing subjective about the former.

In my opinion we see the aura emitted by the body with the rods, or principally with the rods.

The aura is always grey or blue. It is never visible in a strong light. It is not visible in broad daylight.

Although this view has never been previously expressed, I have often wondered whether Kilner had not made the same discovery, if discovery it be, but that he did not realize the cause of it. It must be remembered, though, that Kilner did his experiments more than twenty years ago.

He advises one never to strain the eyes by staring hard at the outline of a body. Since the rods lie to the *side* of the centre part of the retina which is lined solely by cones and which receives the direct image of the object being viewed, it would, if I am right, clearly be an advantage to look at the object, if not out of the corner of one's eye, at least not be peering hard and directly at it. This can easily be tested. Pick out some small object such as one of the dimmest stars at night, and look *at* it hard. Then look just to the side of it. You will see it much the more easily in the latter case.

Kilner also says that the aura does not always appear at once. *The rods function more slowly than the cones do*, in any case, and especially when they have been exhausted by the presence of a bright light. When one goes out into the night from a brightly lit room at first one can see nothing. The reason is that the cones will not be stimulated by the dim light, and the rods, which have been exhausted by the bright one, recover but slowly.

Again, if the light is bright the iris muscles will have contracted the pupil of the eye until it is too small for rays of light to strike that part of the retina where the rods are situated. It is only in a dim light that the pupil is extended sufficiently for the rods to be brought into play.

If we stare hard at any particular object the image of it will fall on the fovea centralis, the centre of the retina, which is thinned here by the fact that all layers except the outermost one have gradually disappeared.

In the fovea centralis all the rods have disappeared so that it is lined not only entirely by cones, but by cones bigger than those found in any other part of the retina.

As one passes from this central part to the periphery of the retina it will be found that the proportion of cones decreases while that of rods increases until, finally, one reaches that part that lies but a short way behind the ciliary muscles which pull on the back of the lens to alter its convexity. Here only rods are to be found.

The fovea centralis is not more than 1·5 mm. in diameter, which represents a visual angle of 6° at the most. Only between this angle, therefore, is really clear vision possible at any particular moment. The sensations which are excited by the stimulation of the more marginal part of the retina will be less distinct than those excited by the image on the fovea.

Now since the fovea contains vastly more cones than it does rods, I maintain that the image of the ultra-violet aura will never be formed upon this central spot, and so will never come into the angle of direct vision.

The rods secrete a purple fluid, *visual purple*, or *rhodopsin*. If a frog is kept in the dark for some time before being killed, it will be found on removing the eye that its retina will be of a purple colour—provided that the dissection is carried out in a weak light. This colour will be found upon examination under the microscope to be restricted to the rods alone. It will be noticed also that it very soon disappears upon exposure to daylight. Any bright light, in fact, bleaches it.

That rhodopsin enables the rods to see rays of ultra-violet wave-length is possible. By means of it photographs can be taken upon the retina of an eye that has been removed, though, of course, the image would be an inverted one since the eye is no longer connected with the brain.

In a human eye there are some three million cones, as opposed to eighteen million rods.

Schultz many years ago told us that in the retina of such animals as the owl and the cat the rods are very much more numerous than the cones, which are more or less absent. Since the rods are not affected by red rays and are probably stimulated by ultra-violet ones, I suggest that the aura emitted by a living mouse, like that of man, consists in the main of ultra-violet rays and not of infra-red ones. It is difficult to discover exactly where in the solar spectrum these ultra-violet rays lie, presumably in the near ultra-violet country. Professor Meldola examined with a prism the light emitted by a glow-worm and he found it to belong to quite a narrow region in the middle of the visible spectrum, and to contain no red rays at all. Professor Young, of America, examined the light from an American fire-fly and came to the conclusion that the rays it emitted were situated between the short end of the red and the middle of the blue. Very well chosen on the part of the fire-fly, if I may say so. Plenty of visible light, but very little energy expended.

Presuming that our aura lies in the near ultraviolet, then, let us see how the retina will be affected. Since the aura cannot be seen in bright light, it cannot be seen by the cones. Its light is not sufficiently intense to stimulate them. I have already pointed out that the aura becomes more obvious if viewed by the part of the retina that lies outside the fovea centralis, and that it appears to fade if stared at, i.e. it cannot be seen by the cones of the fovea centralis. Repeating my theory that the aura is perceived by the rods, here is corroborative evidence, since the rods would be exhausted by a bright light. They can appreciate this emission which does not stimulate the cones. The visible spectrum as regards the rods seems not to coincide exactly with that of the cones. Although the rods see everything as blue-grey, they can just pick up these rays in the near ultraviolet.

CHAPTER VII

COMPLEMENTARY COLOURS

IT is difficult to ignore this side of the problem entirely. Others have set great store on the help obtained in seeing the aura through the use of complementary colours. May I say from the beginning that I set no very great store on this or upon any other help which is purely of a subjective nature—and this is subjective, nothing more.

Here is a very brief appreciation of the theory : We have agreed that looking for a long time at one particular colour causes fatigue to the nerve endings that are sensitive to that colour. Temporary blindness to that colour results. Similarly other shades that include that colour will be affected. Thus purple to the red blind eye will appear blue, and to the blue blind eye will look red—since purple, being the colour complementary of green, is made up entirely of blue and red. Strips of paper or talc made in the various colours required will help to bring about the desired effect.

Suppose one looks at red, or through such a strip of red paper, and then transfers one's gaze on to a white screen upon which rays of purple light are being thrown, the result should be that purple light would appear at least a bluey purple if not pure blue.

While temporarily blind to one of the three primary colours, the eye is hypersensitive to the other two. Also the shades of the other two in a mixture are picked out with greater clearness. Hence, if one looks through a *yellow* strip, since yellow is the complementary colour of blue (being a mixture of green and red), all the colour nerves are fatigued except the blue ones. Thus the eye becomes hypersensitive for the time being to blue—and so, to violet which is ultra-blue.

In young people violet may be a primary colour ; that is to say, one of the three colours produced by chemical action of the neurones of the retina. These primary colours will in all probability begin by being violet, green and red. In later years they may have changed to blue, yellow and red. My own might still, I believe, truthfully be called violet, green and red. The violet to blue will usually be the first change, then the green will tend to go yellow-wards. The red does not vary.

In consequence, so will the shades of the complementary colours change. As already referred to, the colour which one person calls canary may not be the same colour as that so designated by another. Again, as one gets older, the colour canary will be obtained by using different proportions of green and red, until finally canary becomes almost one of the primary colours.

We have now arrived at the following deductions : (1) Dicyanin *sensitizes*. (2) The yellow strips of paper cut out the red and the greens, thus making the eye particularly sensitive to blue.

These two statements should be kept quite separate. The latter is merely a subjective effect, and therefore of far less importance. It need not be ignored, nevertheless. Often much help has been obtained when inspecting the aura, particularly in pathological cases. For example, owing to some derangement, such as disease of an organ, a patch appears in the aura. Perhaps the patch will be very faint, little more than a suspicion such as might result from imperfect lighting or from a darker shadow being cast upon one side of the subject than upon the other. If the subject turns round—and the patch moves too, then it is clearly no suspicion and every device must be resorted to in order to clarify it. It may lead to a hitherto unsuspected disease's being diagnosed.

Let me say again that the colour of the aura is always some shade of blue-grey, but with the aid of these coloured strips sometimes a patch in the aura shows up more clearly. Some will say, I know, that since such effects are merely of a subjective nature, one is no longer dealing with genuine emissions from the body of the subject undergoing inspection, but with phantom images created in one's own eye. True, *but* phantom images cannot be formed without a background. Here the background is obviously the aura.

If, for example, a certain organ is diseased it will not emit an aura of the same brightness as that emitted by the rest of the body. Although this might be difficult to locate with any certainty in many cases, the use of such complementary coloured strips and their phantom images may be of great assistance, for there will of necessity be a gap in such a phantom where the aura is missing. Where such a gap, or patch, appears and, after one has satisfied oneself that it is not due to any defect in lighting, still persists, it suggests very strongly indeed that something is wrong. The aura is quite a stable thing and is emitted, under normal conditions, with more or less equal brightness all over the body. If, therefore, some part fails to emit an aura there must be a cause of such a failure. Often one finds brighter patches, due to pregnancy, for instance, but very rarely duller ones—unless something is wrong.

It is in the diagnosis of disease that these complementary coloured strips help to turn suspicion into something stronger.

Now comes the question as to which is the most useful of these complementary coloured strips. Undoubtedly the answer is that most help will be rendered by the yellow strip, yellow being the complementary colour of blue—the colour of the aura is always blue-grey, either because we see it with our rods or because we are seeing some colour of shorter wave-length than that of violet. Also, as we are endeavouring to see into the ultra-violet we want to eliminate reds and greens of which colours yellow is the mixture. By using this yellow strip we, therefore, fatigue our eyes to yellow, i.e. to red and green. Blue, as a result, is seen the more easily. Dicyanin is blue, but the dye is a *sensitizer*. It enables us to see the aura, which is objective fact, while the phantom images caused by fatigue are merely subjective.

The natural shade of yellow required by a particular eye must be a question for the individual. This must depend to some extent on the exact shade of the primary colour produced by the stimulation of the blue-sensitive nerves. These, as has been pointed out, will vary slightly with age.

Presuming that the three primary colours are red, green and blue-violet, then the following will be some complementary tints—I call them tints for they are merely colours by mixture.

Scarlet (primary colour) . .	Peacock
Green (primary colour) . .	Magenta
Blue-violet (primary colour) .	Yellow
Violet (purple) . . .	Primrose
Crimson	Jade Green
Orange	Cambridge Blue

This will, at least, give an idea as to what is meant by a complementary colour. The two complements together make up white, i.e. Blue+Green+Red. White is made up of all the primary colours, and so requires no complement. One might consider black as the complement of white, just as an " angle " of 0° is the complementary angle of a right angle.

Artistic people will tell us which colours contrast or blend with which, by their experience. The study of the eye and complementary colours will give us the answer also. Black and white are obvious contrasts. So, too, are blue and yellow or, for a matter of that, any other pair of complementary colours.

Let us try. Let us take some fairly out-of-the-way shade. Mauve ? Say, pale mauve, or lilac. Here we are up against a difficulty, perhaps, since some will disagree that pale mauve is anything like lilac. Let us call this colour the one produced when a potassium salt is placed in the edge of a bunsen flame. Our colour lies somewhere between the primary colours, red and blue. It is light magenta, but nearer over towards blue. Its complement will, therefore, be dark green—bottle green—with just a suggestion of yellow. Sky blue, which to me is lighter than, and not so green as, turquoise, will be the complement of very dark yellow, tending rather towards red than green—i.e. brown.

CHAPTER VIII

THE OUTER HAZE AND SEX

IT was mentioned in Chapter I that women make better subjects for the study of the aura than do men or children.

I have found, and I think that others will agree with me, that the light surrounding a child is more compact than the haze described as the average aura which from the point of view of the investigator might be termed that of a healthy female adult of fair intellect.

In the case of the child, of either sex, the inside aura is much as that described. It is in the outer haze that the difference occurs.

While the woman's outer haze extends for some distance beyond the brighter inside aura, finally fading away at its distal margin, that of a child is perhaps brighter, though appreciably less bright than the inside aura, and the further edge is more distinct. The width of the haze is about twice that of the inside aura ; that is to say, it extends a similar distance beyond it, each part being some three inches wide. It is of

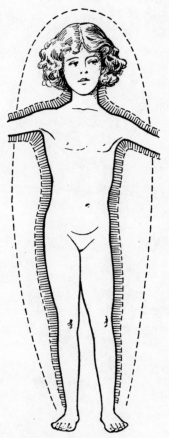

Child, showing narrow outer haze.

less interest than the haze emitted by a woman, not only because it is narrower, but also because the effects of external forces upon it are much less marked. It, too, is less sensitive in registering internal changes, either natural or pathological.

Let us consider the change from the juvenile type of haze to that of the adult. In the case of the male the change is but small, but with women the alteration is a gradual one, just as the change from the childish figure to the fuller and more mature curves is. The transitional stage in each case occupies several years. There is perhaps this difference : the aura does not begin to change as a rule before puberty, rarely in fact before the age of fourteen years. Again, the fully extended adult haze is not to be found much before nineteen. Of course, there are exceptions, many of them, but this fact suggests that there is a connexion between puberty and the alteration in shape of the aura, and also that if there is some connexion, then puberty would seem to be the cause and the transitional aura the effect.

The aura may be used to aid diagnosis of disease, but the disease must come first and the registration follow. In many cases, though, the disease may be long-standing and even deeply rooted before it makes itself evident. Again, it is easy to imagine cases where the symptoms have led to a wrong diagnosis. An examination of the aura may then prove very helpful indeed. Just as conditions of health cause the aura to change in shape, texture and colour, so too will natural changes, metamorphosis shall we say, make their influence felt—puberty, menstruation, pregnancy, to mention some of the more obvious. Soon after the onset of puberty the outer haze begins to extend its distal margin as we have said, becoming possibly fainter and taking on a less definite shape. Shortly before a menstrual period becomes due the haze may become brighter in the neighbourhood of the mammary glands and possibly in front of the throat. To appreciate these signs, which are not very obvious, the subject should be viewed from the side instead of facing the observer.

These somewhat subtle changes may be noticed a day or so before the menstrual period makes itself known ; it should be remembered that the change begins in the sexual organs very considerably before it becomes obvious—still, then, the change in the aura is the effect and not the cause. The aura is, let me repeat, an outward sign of an inward cause—no, not a spiritual sign, even, just physical and quite unromantic, and not in the least mystic.

Pregnancy, too, leaves its mark, and here I feel this little off-the-beaten-track branch of scientific research may prove its worth.

As might be expected, it is the outer haze that is principally affected. The sexual organs, going back to our earthworm again, lie in the space between the skin and the digestive tract, and we are assuming that the haze has its origin in the mesoderm and the ectoderm. "Am I pregnant?" a question the general practitioner is so often up against. A woman has missed a period; perhaps it is only a few days late. It is a difficult question to answer. The condition of the aura may prove helpful. (1) Over the mammary glands, in all probability, the haze will be wider as well as deeper— I think deeper describes its appearance better than brighter. A similar condition would be expected if the menstrual period was delayed, but in this case it should arrive in the course of a couple of days. (2) A widening of the haze, to no great extent at first, but none the less discernible, may be expected in front of the area from the navel to the pubes. As time goes on this occurrence will become more marked and, as the time of birth approaches, the inside aura will appear wider, more stripey and brighter, no doubt owing to the creation of the baby's aura. In the one case that I have run across where it was suspected that the unborn child was dead this change in the inside aura was absent, except for the additional striation. The suspicion was later confirmed. However, one case is not much to draw conclusions from. I am not a doctor, so my opportunities of inspecting such cases are extremely few. A fact that applies equally to pathological cases. Artists' models are well built and healthy and invariably possess average healthy auras, but such present as a rule no features of especial interest.

A slight decrease in clearness of the aura in general often accompanies pregnancy in the *early* stages, presumably due to its somewhat upsetting effect upon the general health of the subject. This phenomenon, however, does not persist as the condition of pregnancy advances. Certain reflex actions of the sexual organs have their origin in the lumbar or sacral area of the spinal cord. Kilner mentions a dark patch in the aura of a healthy woman here when viewed from the side. He alleges that the disappearance of this patch is an additional argument in favour of diagnosing pregnancy. I feel rather

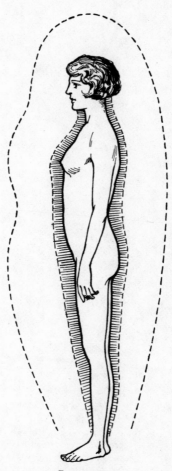

Pregnant aura.

that the patch—which I have, of course, noticed over this region—may be due to lateral attraction of the rays here owing to the arch of the back, the fact that it is concave, and the aura emitted by it, instead of running directly away from the body at right angles, is inclined to be attracted either upwards or downwards, thus leaving a suggestion of a void at this place. The patch is more obvious in the *inside* aura than in the haze beyond, and its tendency to disappear in pregnancy is possibly due merely to the filling out of the hollow, for the uterine mucous membrane swells rapidly in pregnant women, attaining a thickness of $\frac{1}{2}$ cm. within a fortnight. Obviously a very slight increase of internal pressure will make a marked difference in the concavity of the small of the back. If my theory of the aura's origin is correct, the change should be registered on the outer haze rather than on the inside material aura, since this latter has its origin in the endoderm.

The slight effect noticed in the outer haze I attribute to nervous influence of this part of the spine. Goltz quotes an experiment in the case of a bitch whose cord had been divided in the thoracic region a year previously. She came on heat (which we may take to be synonymous with menstruation) at the proper time and also became pregnant. On the other hand, if the cord is destroyed at the lumbo-sacral region all reflex action of the uterus is prevented. Clearly this part of the spine is the centre of control of some of the sexual functions, and may easily be responsible for the slight change which some-times (not always) occurs in the outer haze in cases of pregnancy.

I have found the widening of the haze emitted by the mammary glands the safest indication of pregnancy in early stages. This widening seems to indicate a normal menstrual period missed. I do not, however, think that one can diagnose pregnancy with any degree of certainty in very early days.

The growth of the mammary glands during pregnancy is to a large extent due to hormone action set up in the ovary, and later in the baby. Some beginning of action in these glands may take place even with menstruation, since the corpus luteum (which is the tissue that the ovary produces when it sheds the ovum) and the milk glands are inter-connected. Even sexual intercourse may have some very slight influence upon the breasts, but this is short lived. I mention this to illustrate the difficulty experienced in determining whether pregnancy has taken place or not.

After a fortnight the chief difficulties will have been removed, for the mammary glands will have resumed normal conditions by then unless further stimulated by a gland in the wall of the uterus, which would not have made its appearance felt until a fortnight had elapsed.

CHAPTER IX

THE OUTER HAZE AND THE NERVOUS SYSTEM

IT has been mentioned in an earlier chapter that the outer haze varies in colour from pale grey to a bright blue. The better the intellect of the subject the bluer the haze. I have never seen any colour in human beings other than these, except in pathological cases when dark patches sometimes occur.

In the case of a coloured man the aura is not, perhaps, a real grey. There is a decidedly brownish tinge about it; the texture, too, is much coarser than that of the aura of a European.

Texture varies considerably—possibly this may be hereditary. I have not been able to inspect sufficient numbers of auras of members of the same family to form an opinion that would be of any real value. I have, however, noticed a marked similarity between the texture of the hazes of people who are related to one another. I will deal with the connexion between texture and heredity more fully later.

The outer haze in the case of animals, it is, I think, only reasonable to suppose, would exist to a much lower degree of development than that of man. Since, to some extent, brightness seems to register intellect, and shape is under the control of the nervous system, one would not expect the outer haze to be as prominent as it is in the case of ourselves. Perhaps that is why I have not been able to use animals as subjects with any degree of success up to now. Also, it would not be surprising if their hazes turned out to be of a darker colour.

I am unable to account for my not being able to see some sort of an inside aura, though. It may, of course, be narrower than ours, but in animals such as the domestic cat I should have expected it to be considerable. It has been suggested that it may possibly be found to have an infra-red wave-length. *Possibly* this may be so, but it is difficult to believe that no auras happen to have a wave-length of visible light. Why should some be too long to see and others be too short ? Surely some would be visible to the normal eye ?

Now for a few words as regards the shape of the outer haze. Wherever a subject enjoying good health has been examined, the inside aura has been bright and the haze beyond it has been symmetrical, the general shape, especially in women, being roughly oval. Literally egg-shaped, the round end being above the head, where the outer haze is fairly wide, widening still further as far as the waist and then tapering not too rapidly towards the feet.

Outer auras that fall away suddenly in the neighbourhood of the femur almost invariably belong to people who are suffering from some nervous complaint, or who at least have such a tendency.

When viewed sideways the outer haze emitted from the dorsal side, that is to say, in the neighbourhood of the spine, though not following the curve of the waist above the buttocks as the inside aura does, should not bulge outwards. Whether the subject has a rounded back or not, the outer haze should not have one—such a shape indicates a tendency towards hysteria, for certain.

People with a neurotic tendency almost invariably have a poor haze beyond their inside aura. Not necessarily a particularly grey one, but narrow and faint. The inside aura, too, usually lacks lustre. The whole appearance might be described, as might the subjects themselves, perhaps, as listless. Indefinite may

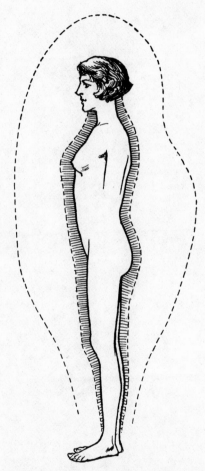

Neurotic aura showing dorsal bulge and tapering towards ankles.

be a better word. The differentiation between the two parts of the aura is indefinite. The distal margin is also indefinite. Of course, the haze *gradually* fades away in the case of the most splendidly healthy aura, but there is a very great difference. In the latter case the haze is wide and seems almost to glow ; in the former it is narrow, faint and—just listless ! It suggests the very opposite to blooming health.

I think I may say that the outer haze nearly always extends further on the dorsal side than on the ventral, except perhaps in cases of pregnancy when, as I have mentioned, a wider haze may be seen in the neighbourhood of the abdomen, especially as the time for deliverance draws near. Under ordinary circumstances the haze is wider on the dorsal side ; the reason presumably is that one of the sources of origin is the spinal cord.

A case where the spine had been damaged causing paralysis of both legs, the aura emitted below the point of damage was negligible.

Another case, however, where a boy in his early twenties had sustained damage to his brain from gunshot over the left temple, although his right arm was useless, it was surrounded by a haze—a poor one, it is true, nevertheless the haze was emitted. Perhaps this will diminish gradually, for one could not surely hold out any hopes of the arm's ever regaining its use, since the damage was to the brain.

I do not know details of the damage, nor do I know exactly what operation was performed. I had no opportunity of enquiring. I knew him fairly well, in fact I had stayed at his home, but he had invited me there to play cricket and I did not feel justified in broaching the subject —no doubt a painful one to him—though I must admit that I should have liked to have known more. I do not meet such cases very often and, unless one has a full knowledge of the operation performed, the importance that one can attach to such a case must obviously deteriorate. I should have expected, however, that the haze would have been a much fainter one than it was, though in neither of these cases were there facilities for making a proper inspection. I shall not allow their evidence to weigh unduly for, unless the subject is put through a thorough examination under specially prepared conditions, the conclusions arrived at ought not to be. Clearly such results are more or less useless. I have on several occasions properly examined hands from which fingers have been amputated. In no case has there been an aura

emitted from the missing part of such a finger—
naturally. Any more than there could be an
aura emitted by a dead body in a place where
the body is not. When ghosts go a-hunting,
the spectres seen by the eyes of the living are
not auras in our sense—viz. rays emitted by the
body—whatever else they may be.

Of course, these hands have always been the
hands of friends of Army days, whose mutila-
tions have been of some years' standing. I
realize that point. There is no aura surrounding an amputated limb neither after its removal
from the body nor in the place which it had
previously occupied. I do not expect that,
because a finger is comparatively a small
member, or yet because it is a pointed projection, it could leave behind its aura after it had
lost the power of emitting one. This, to my
mind, is impossible. I have examined a nerve
which had been laid bare in a dissecting-room ;
the body had been long since dead, and very
naturally there was no aura to be seen. Neither
was there one from a similar brain. I mention
this to stress my point that the aura is emitted
by the living body and not merely from certain
tissue, alive or dead.

It has been stated that when a living body is
subjected to a charge of electricity such as

might be imparted by a Wimshurst machine, the inside aura fades and then returns much expanded. I have tried the effect of a similar charge upon a dead nerve, incidentally the one laid bare in the dissecting-room, still there was no aura to be seen. *A fortiori* nothing can be seen surrounding a charged inorganic body. The electric field surrounding an inanimate object cannot be seen as an aura. This seems to bear out my statement that the outer haze runs beneath the inside aura ; the electrically charged particles are not of themselves visible without the presence of the ultra-violet rays. Neither have I been able to pick up ultra-violet rays from sunlight by means of my sensitizing screen.

The living body seems to possess some power of fluorescence, that of picking up rays of white light and emitting shorter ones of ultra-violet wave-length. Usually fluorescent bodies re-emit rays of a longer wave-length than that of those originally received.

The screen, in like manner, picks up these ultra-short waves which on passing through the dye become visible. This, however, is not quite a true description of the function of the dye used in my screen, for its effect is upon the eye rather than upon the rays. The eye is sensitized so that it can appreciate rays of shorter wave-length than it can normally appreciate. Some part of the eye must undergo temporary change—we have threshed out the possibilities, and have decided that no change of refractive index is possible as such, but that the effect must be upon the nerve endings of the retina itself. I have suggested that this sensitizing makes itself felt upon the rods, perhaps by increasing the secretion of visual purple. This and a certain amount of fluorescence performed by the albuminous tissue through which rays pass on their way through the eye to the retina, seem to be the most probable explanations. The first, an effect upon the nervous tissue of the eye, and the second, a lengthening of the wave-length of the rays due to fluorescence, which change is perceived by the rod nerve-endings.

CHAPTER X

THE EFFECT OF DISEASE ON THE OUTER HAZE

IT has been pointed out that much more research will be necessary before one can name with any degree of certainty the sources of the inside aura. In dealing with the sources of the outer haze the wicket plays much more true ; there are comparatively few instances of conflicting evidence, whereas everything points to the nervous system as the principal agent, intellect controlling the colour (blue=good, grey=not so good), shape and brightness being affected to some extent by disease, while sexual disorders are registered upon the width.

It is quite impossible to lay down anything hard and fast, there would be too many modifications if I did, but certain disorders are almost invariably indicated by their own sets of signs : People who have neurotic tendencies, are emotional, hysterical or even just nervy, are sure to have the dorsal bulge in their outer haze. The haze will possibly be rather indistinct and may taper away quickly towards the ankles. In definite cases of epileptic trouble both the bulge and the decrease of the haze towards the ankles will probably be well marked. The shape of the haze will alter from time to time as the physical conditions of the subject improve or decline. Apart from the dorsal bulge and this tendency to narrow from the femur downwards, sexual disturbances play the principal part in the control of shape.

Brightness of the outer haze seems to vary directly as fitness, to the extent that " strong nerves " are usually indicated by a bright, distinct haze. Men very often have clear, bright hazes though the width may be only three or four inches. The " nervous wreck " may have a wide haze, particularly in the case of a woman, but her haze will in all probability be dull and will show the bulge and tapering referred to. Colour seems to depend on intellect only. However fit physically the subject may be, it is unlikely that the haze emitted will be blue. Very fine specimens of men physically will have good, clear auras, but they may be grey ones. Since the haze emitted by a coloured man is grey with a suggestion of brown about it, it follows that the aura of an animal should be of a duller hue than the human pale grey. It could not be blue, of course. One would expect it to be darker than the human grey, and probably less conspicuous, which perhaps accounts for my being unable to locate it, though I have not at present given it much serious attention owing to my being unable to obtain suitable subjects, as I have pointed out. The presence of hair would probably obliterate the inside aura, and may possibly cover up part of the outer haze in some instances, for I should not expect to find a very wide or clear haze. I have suggested that a cat might be expected to have a good inside aura—by this I mean a bright one, for the inside aura is never very wide—but a cat's fur would be of sufficient length to interfere seriously with clear vision even under the best conditions. Sick animals are much more easy to come by than sick humans unless one is in medical practice. One's opportunities of inspecting, thoroughly inspecting, what I may term pathological auras are decidedly limited. Unless there have been facilities for looking at an aura under the best conditions the information gleaned and the opinion arrived at will be respectively scanty and insecure. A thorough investigation, one that will be at all worth while, must necessarily be carried out with the knowledge and the help of the subject. By saying that the subject can herself help, I mean that she can help by not hindering, just as when one visits a dentist it is helpful to keep one's mouth open and one's tongue still—and civil. Personally, I have found that a general relaxing of the brain on the part of the subject is helpful. Thinking of nothing, or should I say of nothing in particular, is preferable to any attempt at concentration. Others have said that by concentration the appearance of the aura can be altered—its intensity increased and its colour changed. Perhaps this may be the case with clairvoyants and geniuses, but I feel sure that even the greatest of these will admit, if only to themselves, that they have never gained very much advantage by concentrating on a colour. The leopard is spotted, and spotted he will remain—at least until he changes his ways and his surroundings, and such changes must be very gradual. So with the aura which must, I feel, be blue or grey though it may change from one shade of blue-grey to another gradually, varying with the intellect or mental health of the subject. Concentration upon certain colours is claimed to improve health or to ward off danger, presumably by the subject's becoming encysted in his or her aura. All very suggestive of faith healing, I fear. Put on a halo and you become a good man. Yet perhaps by dressing the part you may be able to act it the better. Was it not Coué who advised one to say : " Every day in every way I am getting better and better " ? The degree of betterness in this case applied to progress along the pathway to health, not heaven, though. Seriously, one can no doubt by concentration affect the nerves locally—partly through the imagination, possibly. I cannot agree from my own observations that one can affect the colour of one's aura by concentrating one's thoughts upon it.

I have noticed, however, that people who " haven't a nerve in their body," the kind that are not easily ruffled, have more compact outer hazes very often than jumpy or temperamental people. " Strong, silent " people, and let us include " quiet little men " in this category, generally have narrow hazes which are often bright ; the more emotional type of person has a wider aura. The suggestion is that the aura in the latter case is under less control than in the former—that it has been allowed to wander, so to speak ; given more latitude. I offer no substantiating evidence in favour of this view. It is too " abstract " to be explained scientifically, at least until more detail has been collected with regard to it. Possibly in days to come we may be justified in remonstrating with someone who is out of temper : " Do try to keep your aura under control." Also, people who may be described as scatter-brained or as being unable to concentrate sometimes have wide outer auras. These people are often nervy, and so have the usual dorsal bulge, or unrestricted haze, in the region of the nerve cord. Nervous disorders we have shown do register themselves upon the outer haze, though local disease of an ectodermal nature does not appear in such a marked fashion on this part of the aura as does definite disease of what I have termed an endodermal nature upon the inside aura. The inside aura is itself more marked, more definite, than the haze beyond it, with the result that any gap, or void, in it caused by a diseased organ's not emitting an aura would very naturally be more easily noticed. General debility, being out of sorts, does tend to dim the haze. A person who is run down will probably have a dull haze. If the degree of run down-ness amounts to a nervous breakdown, the haze may extend, becoming very indistinct and having no definite distal boundary. This haze appears to be a more sensitive instrument than the inside aura which, although it changes in degree of brightness, varies very little in width in men, women or children whether they be fit or ill—but the colour, I contend, will always be blue-grey. Kilner claims that women can change the colour of their auras at will and that the colours so produced " unquestionably do not belong to the ordinary visible solar spectrum." He suggests that they belong to a second and higher spectrum of shorter wave-lengths. Somehow or other, it would appear that the rays forming the aura were capable of stimulating his cones, at any rate at times.

Ultra-violet rays can affect disease, for example, rickets can be caused by a lack of vitamin A in the diet. This condition can be lessened by ultra-violet rays, the reason being perhaps that the rays increase the vitamin in the body by releasing it.

Ultra-violet rays will produce sterilization and will destroy certain bacteria. Thus, if these short-waved rays can affect disease, surely it is reasonable to expect that the presence of disease in a body should register itself upon the emission of such rays ? In short, disease should, and does, make its presence known by an examination of the aura.

Unfortunately these health-bringing rays from the sun do not reach us in as large proportions as might be expected, one reason being, as I have pointed out earlier, the fact that our own atmosphere stops them. Ultraviolet rays turn oxygen into ozone—a reason for there being more ozone in the upper air than near the earth.

Carbon dioxide and nitrogen are nearly transparent to ultra-violet rays, the prohibiting element being oxygen. Evidence shows that it is oxygen, in the form of ozone actually, which is responsible for limiting the solar spectrum of these rays. I believe it was Lord Rayleigh who said that the lower air is far more transparent for ultra-violet rays than that of the upper regions, the inference being that the comparatively greater proportion of ozone there prevents their passage earthwards.

The effect of ultra-violet rays upon living beings may be summed up briefly thus :

(*a*) Stimulative—those of longer wavelength, i.e. those nearer to the visible part of the spectrum.

(*b*) Lethal—those of shorter wave-length which lie further away.

The abiotic, or lethal, are those with a wave-length of less than 305 $\mu\mu$.

Burge told us that rays with wave-lengths between 302 and 254 $\mu\mu$ exert a chemical effect upon protoplasm, changing living cells into an insoluble compound, or coagulum.

Radiations between 296 and 210 $\mu\mu$ are absorbed by skin of thickness of one millimetre, but the longer ultra-violet rays, those that have wave-lengths between 380 and 296 $\mu\mu$, have no effect on germs, 294 to 238 $\mu\mu$ being approximately the germicide range. These render atoxic the toxin of diphtheria, for example.

It is, perhaps, a little curious that man has no sensory organs for detecting ultra-violet radiations. We have no nervous apparatus to receive impressions from rays that are intense enough to be harmful and yet too feeble to make their presence felt by conversion into heat. Woodruff suggests that our remote ancestors evolved in cloudy, dark regions where ultra-violet rays existed in very small quantities indeed and that for this reason no such nerve sense was necessary and so did not evolve. During later stages of evolution protective pigment developed. It was then too late to evolve a new nerve sense by variation.

The ultra-violet rays from the sun lie between 400 and 290 $\mu\mu$, that is to say, they are all in the near region of longer waves. They are not, therefore, of themselves in the lethal country, but they just run into it at the extreme short boundary. Probably the sun's heat helps to make them potent enough to destroy certain bacteria. The mid region, 300 to 200 $\mu\mu$, is powerfully germicidal. These are the rays emitted by the quartz mercury arc. The rays of shorter length still are very naturally situated in a comparatively unknown country, especially beyond 150 $\mu\mu$.

Many insects should, and do, suffer from the effects of ultra-violet radiations. White ants when in search of food travel by subway so as to avoid the sun's rays ; other insects postpone their rambles abroad till the sun has set.

Many molluscs, too, find the sun's radiations more than they can cope with. Of course, in some cases the trouble is merely the heat, while in others it is the light, for example our owl. To the lower animals, though, the rays of shorter wave-length are in many cases the danger, their skins unless specially protected by pigment or other means absorb the sun's ultra-violet waves. As I have said, our skins afford us good protection ; even so, rays that do us no harm may prove lethal to other creatures. Wasp grubs have to be sealed up in light-proof cells if they are to survive and reach maturity.

Schanz says that the principal function of colour in flowers is the selection of the radiations required in each particular case. Perhaps our aura is re-emitted from the appropriate layers of the body, possibly, even, without much alteration in wave-length, which amounts to little more than reflexion, though not from the surface of the skin, of course. It is contrary to experience to suppose that any form of fluorescence is brought about, in that none of the rays are lengthened into visible light on being re-emitted. The rays making up the outer haze are, I believe, in the near ultra-violet country, probably only just beyond the visible part of the spectrum.

CHAPTER XI

THE AURA THROUGH THE EYES OF ANIMALS

THE eyes of the owl, as we have said, consisting of rods but having no cones, must be unable to appreciate colour as well as being practically useless as organs of vision during the day-time. This is, of course, fairly obvious, from his habit of keeping out of the way of other animals during the bright hours. The sunlight would instantly exhaust his rods, rendering him powerless against the onslaught of even the most diminutive bird, his eyes being, in fact, specially attuned to his nocturnal hunting.

Imagine him flying well above the ground on the look-out for food, not just a few inches up, peering into nook and cranny for a possible supper—or should we say breakfast ? Clearly, mice are easy enough for him to distinguish, and the reason, it seems to me, is, as I have suggested, that the aura of ultra-violet rays emitted by the living mouse makes it an obvious target, an object conspicuous indeed. Little birds, too, know that the owl must be left severely alone at night. They also emit their aura, to their undoing. The owl does not rely upon the trick common to so many other birds of prey of hovering above his victims, frightening them into crouching and thus becoming " sitters," so to speak. This hunter likes to perch upon a post and wait like a cat over a mouse hole—dangerous things, these posts, as keepers put traps on top of them, traps being inanimate objects have no aura, of course, and so the owl falls a victim in his turn. Things like this must be, since the keeper's job is to protect his young pheasants, and owls, like the rest of us, are rather partial to them. The obvious question again : " Perhaps the owl *listens* for his prey, relying upon his ears ? " Birds of prey have ears that are in no way remarkable, neither do they function better by night than by day. Some of the victims utter no cry. Owls like warm-blooded food, we know, but foxes definitely choose frogs and even beetles in preference. This suggests that cold-blooded creatures, too, emit an aura. I agree that this is possible, even probable—fire-flies and glow-worms emit something that is obvious even to us, though there are explanations for this light other than the aura one.

The question of attributing this to smell rather than to sight ? Perhaps ; foxes have good noses though I should not count a beetle among the easiest of animals to wind—frogs, too, having no perineal gland, the organ supplying scent and peculiar to mammals, must be difficult to trace in this manner. Foxes wind chicken, no doubt, for birds have preening glands containing an oil which leaves a distinct and very helpful scent, as any gun dog could tell you. Foxes enjoy killing chicken, though their weak digestions object to their making a hot meal unless there is every opportunity of sleeping it off. A vixen will take birds home—after all, cubs have to be taught what various types of food smell like. I am not pretending that a fox hates fowl ; of course he doesn't, but it becomes definitely out of season when hunting is not, for the fox is himself a hunting animal and knows all the tricks, so is hardly likely to allow himself to be caught out of condition. Horses, too, probably have monochromatic vision, everything looking of the same colour to them, perhaps of a brown tint. Their rods have not fully developed into cones, for the cone is a specialized type of rod that has become acclimatized to bright light and is for that reason to be found on that part of the retina upon which bright light falls, i.e. on the fovea centralis. It is agreed that the early eye consisted of rod neurones only, the cones being evolved later from the rods.

Horses dislike large objects that seem to them to be unusual, especially if they are at the side of the road where they can be viewed with only one eye and, therefore, cannot be seen in perspective. Most of us know how nervous some horses are when passing objects such as a fallen tree by the roadside, how easily too can a fox be headed or a rabbit be turned when he is bolting from corn that is being cut. Farmers will shout when a rabbit is making for the hedge and safety, with the result that the rabbit will turn back into the field. Shouting is, of course, accompanied by waving of sticks, the latter being far more effective than the former, though rabbits are easily flurried by a noise and thrown into a panic—and rabbits are not the only animals that can be stampeded ! Most creatures that live in crowds easily become scared because one of their number is frightened—cows, deer of all sorts, horses, even elephants, and some of them, once on the run, will cause their pursuers many a weary—and a wary—tramp before they will come up with their quarry again.

Surely very few mammals have longer sight than has man. Most of the larger animals in the bush or jungle hunt by scent, while the hunted know that their best protection is to remain absolutely still and to trust to their natural camouflage. Even to us a zebra if standing still is extremely difficult to see, although we are comparatively close to him. The eyes of animals detect movement at once, but not colour, other than lights and darks; natural camouflage must, therefore, be even more effective in helping its owner to elude the majority of animal eyes than human ones.

Owing to their length of snout, the majority of the larger animals have their vision at the side of the head limited to one eye, which means absence of perspective, and so judgment of respective distances of objects by their movement in parallax is curtailed. Only objects in the direct gaze can be definitely placed in terms of their surroundings, while it is also difficult to judge speed correctly when only one eye is being used. The eye has only its one function, sight, but the eyes as a pair may claim the additional one, perspective. In the same way the ears as a pair help each other to detect the direction of a sound. The ear of a mammal is, like all Gaul, divided into three parts. The innermost and oldest part, which controls balance ; the middle, which is responsible for hearing, and the outer ear, which is peculiar to mammals only, for collecting sound. The pinna of a rabbit may be termed an auditory periscope ; it enables him to hear without exposing his head to danger.

With regard to the lower animals, it is very naturally no easy matter to make anything in the nature of a definite statement about their aura, supposing them to emit one. I have not *seen* anything of the kind, unless the light from a glow-worm may be taken as aura, or to be due in part to something that may be defined as such. It is light emitted by a living body. It surely seems more likely that they should emit something in the nature of an aura than that they should not.

I have recently been shown a photograph of an aura around Glastonbury Tor. A haze of a sort there certainly was. These things do happen in photography. I repeat that inanimate objects cannot emit an aura in our sense of the word. Lines, extended outlines following the shape of an object, are often seen. These

are subjective. A trick of our own eyes, sometimes, perhaps, merely due to the two eyes
being momentarily of a different focus. I have
seen this phenomenon referred to as " halination." I cannot consider it as having any
claim whatsoever to being emitted by the
object. Just possibly it may be a type of
phantom image caused by gazing at the object.
It is undoubtedly of a subjective nature and,
as such, it is not an aura. Dare I say that these
" halinations " are hallucinations of the eye ?
After all, since they are merely subjective,
they must be.

I have mentioned the existence of a very
narrow dark band between the skin and the
apparent proximal edge of the inside aura.
This band, which is probably a void in the aura,
has been called the Etheric Double. I do not
attach great importance to its existence, for
I feel that its presence can be accounted for
by what I may call disappointing means. It is
in all probability a void in the aura caused by
the latter's being covered up, or at least inter-
fered with, by hairs from the skin—the etheric
double extends only one-eighth of an inch.

Again particles from the skin would dim the
rays of the aura, causing the appearance of a
dark band. I do *not* believe it to be an optical

illusion, it too nearly coincides with the skin to be a " halination." Kilner considers this etheric double to be wider and more plainly visible in people who have a neurotic tendency. I suggest that the dimming of the aura would probably cause this void to appear wider. Whatever be the cause of it there can be no doubt that the inside aura, and for that matter the haze beyond it, too, must cross over this narrow gap.

If the aura is looked at through a red screen the etheric double appears lighter in colour and slightly striated, the striation being, surely, the rays of the inside aura passing through it. I do not feel that we need attach much importance to this void. It is not easy to see much in one-eighth of an inch of nothingness bounded on one side by solid skin and on the other by a dim haze—for we cannot claim that even the inside aura is much more. Investigation is made less difficult if a white background is used instead of the usual black or crimson one.

Returning to the probable appearance of the aura to the eyes of animals, we must bear in mind that this must be, to some extent, guesswork. This much we can assert with reasonable certainty : Since the animals that we have mentioned have rod neurones as we have, though the cones have not developed to such a degree of efficiency, the main difference in their sight and our own will lie in the distinguishing of colours. Colour belongs to the cones. We have already suggested that the aura, as an ultra-violet phenomenon, is seen by the rods. The aura is always blue-grey. Everything looks blue-grey at night when the rods are being used. Then there is the rod-eyed owl who sees the live mouse but not the dead meat. Let us assume for the time being that I am right about the aura being seen by the rods, and see what we can deduce further.

The aura is seen better in a subdued light than in a bright one. Obviously, since a bright light exhausts the rods. The owl at night, therefore, should see the aura very clearly, having the advantage of being able to gaze directly at it ; his fovea centralis, like the rest of his eye, will consist of rods.

Again, though our cones may be better than those of other eyes, I doubt whether our rods are. Animals that cannot distinguish colour should, therefore, be able to see the aura at least as well as we can.

The visible spectrum may not lie between the same wave-lengths for all eyes, thus the animals whose visible spectrum extends further towards the short or violet end, may see the aura *clearly* always.

The lower animals—insects, for instance—have not very highly developed eyes. Compound eyes consist of an eye stalk the distal end of which is covered by a transparent cuticle. This is divided into square facets, and corresponds to the cornea. Beneath this lies a vitreous substance which refracts, and under that again comes the retinula which encloses the part actually responsible for vision.

Each little " eye " is separated from the next by black pigment so that the actual visual area of each is very much limited. There are no rods and cones. Such eyes are sensitive to light and certain colours may be described as pleasing or displeasing to certain insects—possibly because they are unable to see others. Most insects seem to like white which of course includes all colours and so must include the particular insect's pleasing colour.

Bees like colours at the short end of the visible spectrum—blues and violets. Anything longer than green they fly past, being apparently unattracted.

Butterflies like whites and reds. Moths, flying at night, ignore red—they cannot see it, presumably—though they like yellow and white, colours that show up well in the dark.

Insects that eat pollen, however, visit yellow flowers—pollen is more often of that colour than of any other.

None of these facts seems to throw any light upon the point as to whether there is any aura emitted from flowers, or from plants in general ; I have been unable to see any. It seems unlikely that any such aura would be visible to a vertebrate eye, though this does not necessarily indicate that insects would be unable to pick up some rays of light that our eyes cannot. Symbiosis between plants and insects is in an advanced state of perfection, if I may use such a contradictory term. Plants, on the one hand, have modified some of their floral leaves into nectaries which supply the reward to the visiting insect. Scent, as well as appropriately pleasing colours, advertises the particular brand of nectar, and so attracts the customer. Different insects have different types of apparatus for collecting the nectar. Here again the customer is served—to a degree—for the nectary is so placed that the visiting insect cannot get at it without performing his share in the contract, namely, the transport of pollen. On the other hand, the insect no doubt has met the plant at least half way by suiting his collecting apparatus to better his obtaining his favourite brand of nectar from the particular flowers that supply it.

The point is, just what part does colour play in this mutual attraction? Here only can the aura question enter—the possibility of the emission of rays of a wave-length invisible to human eyes. Most insects, not all, are suitable transport agents for the pollination of some flower. We have said that bees like blues and violets, but not reds and yellows. How about heather, which is pink—pale red? I don't agree. Heather, as every Scotsman knows, is bonny—and purple—or, shall we say, magenta ; i.e. blue plus red, *blue*, that is the point. White heather? The same, plus green. *Blue* plus red plus green. There are exceptions, no doubt, and they are not very difficult to name, but the general rule holds good to such an extent for us to feel reasonably sure that it is more than mere coincidence. Clearly there is something in the idea of animals, in this case insects, having pleasing colours, and colours that do not attract them—I won't go so far as to call these displeasing colours, because probably the insects that are not attracted to them cannot see them.

If flowers are able to colour their petals, may not an emission of rays be extended beyond the flower in the form of an aura ? And, if so, have insects any means of locating and appreciating it ?

Insects, too, may emit rays. Not necessarily ultra-short ones ; possibly rays of wave-length considerably longer than the visible part of the spectrum. There has been no *really* satisfactory explanation as to how some female moths summon the males. When a female of a particularly rare species happens to become shut up in a room or a greenhouse, it will be noticed after some hours that a male, perhaps several males, of this rare species are flying around outside. Possibly there may have been only a dozen or so of them in the whole county. Yet up they come to answer the call. This can hardly come into the aura category, I know, but I fancy we may term it an emission.

You may remember my mentioning those bundles of rays that extend from the proximal margin of the inside aura and run away out beyond the outer haze, not necessarily parallel to the rays of the inside aura but groping out search-light fashion as if heading for some point away outside the aura country altogether. Possibly—only *possibly*—something of this sort may be emitted and picked up after the manner of wireless waves by distant insects.

Interesting experiments have been done with the minute Arthropod water flea, Daphnia : Ultra-violet rays from an arc lamp play on a tank containing these creatures. They swim backwards and forwards in the water. Then a pane of glass is placed in front of the rays, which cuts out all under that of sunlight, 310 $\mu\mu$. The animals come higher up in the water, i.e. nearer the surface. As soon as the glass pane is removed they return to deeper, and darker, water. Similarly those near the glass side of the tank come nearer to the glass when the shorter-lengthed rays are cut off, and recede into the darker area when the pane is taken away.

Cyclops behaves in a similar fashion.

Most of these minute creatures have no real eyes, but eye-spots sensitive to light.

Since the rays of the sun include those of a wave-length as short as 310 $\mu\mu$ in addition to those of visible light and of the longer ultra-violet region, it is likely that many of these, especially those in the neighbourhood of 400 $\mu\mu$, will be affected by fluorescent substances with the result that they will be re-emitted as, I might say " degraded " into, visible light.

Some animal tissues will prove more fluorescent than others ; hence a visible light should be seen surrounding the more fluorescent tissue. This light may be said to be emitted by that tissue. The aura, too, is emitted by the tissues. Artificial rays of ultra-violet wave-length have been found to be so re-emitted by fluorescent tissue.

Let us see which parts of the human body are the most fluorescent : The eye, the blood and the skin act as protective agents against ultra-violet rays. They absorb them and re-emit them as visible light. The sclerotic coat of the eye with its modification, the cornea, fluoresces a bright blue colour, while the pupil remains dark. The whites of the eyes of some animals fluoresce a duller, more yellowy grey. Hard parts of the skin show up more than softer parts. Scurf fluoresces strongly, and patches of eczema and similar skin diseases are discernible. Skin without pigment is more fluorescent than that of coloured people whose auras, too, are of a distinctly muddy grey.

Golden hairs fluoresce ; so do white ones, both of which are easily distinguishable from dark hairs or brown ones. Artificial blondes do not fluoresce.

Tendons and ligaments fluoresce more than

muscles, while bones appear even more brightly illuminated.

Decayed tissue does not fluoresce.

Of course the intensity of the sun's ultra-violet rays upon the body is very small indeed in comparison with that of the artificial rays which are brought into focus on the body from close range. Hence the fluorescence is far more obvious in the latter deliberate case.

The question arises as to whether we are confusing this fluorescing of rays from various tissue with the aura. Are we ? I think if we look into this fluorescence theory more closely we shall see that the two are very near akin. By each theory ultra-violet rays are emitted by the body—shall we say by the tissues ? It is the same thing. With the artificial lamp the rays are re-emitted as a more obvious glow ; perhaps we may say as light, the colour usually is bluish. In the case of the sun's rays the rays are emitted as ultra-violet rays still, probably lengthened so as to approach more nearly to the wave-length of the visible spectrum. The faint haze emitted—let us say " re-emitted," for the moment—has to be picked up by means of acclimatizing the eyes with specially prepared screens.

The aura is emitted by the body, the constituent parts by different parts of the tissues. Surely this artificial aura in no way damages the aura theory as suggested by my experiments? Rather, I feel that the one supports the other.

It is true that some of the artificially fluoresced rays are not strictly blue or grey, but with so much greater an intensity it is not unnatural that this should be the case. The naturally emitted aura is very difficult to see, and its rays are most certainly still of ultra-violet wavelength. I have never seen them, let me repeat, of any colour other than blue or grey, though sometimes there is just a faint suggestion of a browny tinge about them, as in the case of negroes, or green, as in the case of newly-born white babies. These, however, are still predominantly blue or grey.

Why hypoblastic tissue, the alimentary canal and its glands, should emit rays which, though comparatively bright, do not extend more than some three inches beyond the skin, while rays emitted by the mesoderm and the ectoderm, though less bright, should be seen as an aura some three times that width, is not at present evident. Here, too, is a corroborative reasoning in accordance with my difficulty in being able to see the aura emitted by animals. Since white skins fluoresce more than dark ones, and light hairs more than dark, it is unlikely that much research along these lines will be possible with animals as subjects.

Different emissions will become visible to different eyes. Because an owl can see a mouse, there is no reason why he should see some of the auric emissions which can become visible to the human eye. Conversely, we may be a long way from seeing a mouse's aura. I cannot even hazard a guess at its wave-length, though it must surely be situated somewhere in my ultra-violet country, since the owl's eye consists of rods which cannot see infra-red rays.

I should expect to find this aura somewhere in the long part of the ultra-violet, but attribute my inability to see it rather to lack of intensity than to the shortness of its wave-length.

There are still some pieces of evidence, I am aware, that make me hesitate to reconcile the auric emissions to the fluorescence of the solar ultra-violet rays by tissue. The aura is best inspected in subdued light, for instance, yet my screen has no phosphorescent properties.

I find that it is more difficult to see the aura in dusty areas than in the clearer air at the top of a mountain. Since the ideal medium is a vacuum, it is clear that there would be a greater percentage of ultra-violet rays in sunlight in higher altitudes than at sea-level, where the rays have a longer journey through the earth's atmosphere which is not only correspondingly denser, but contains more particles of dust, etc. This is in accordance with reconciliation to the suggestion that fluorescence by the tissues of the body is at least partly responsible for the emission of the aura.

CHAPTER XII

THE QUESTION OF HEREDITY

AS has already been stated, there has not been much opportunity of making a special study of the auras of several members of one particular family, other than my own, though very naturally certain pronounced characteristics have, so to speak, obtruded themselves. These have been for the most part noticeable in the texture of the aura, a thing very difficult to describe.

When one considers how great are the changes that can be brought about chemically it is easy to realize how some very small foreign influence may cause sufficient variation to outweigh natural heredity.

Variations may be said to be of two kinds : those due to change in the complex of germinal factors and those due to the complex of stimuli of environment. The former is known as mutation and the latter, modification. Both are forms of variation and to look at are indistinguishable.

Modifications will continue to be inherited so long as the stimulus persists. Mutations can be established and passed on from generation to generation, the variation, or change from the normal of the species, becoming more marked by careful selection of parents, e.g. if pigeons with extra-specially puffed-out chests are considered fashionable, show pigeons will be bred only from birds that have this peculiarity pronounced. Here the selection is not natural but artificial, and the mutation is in consequence established after comparatively few generations.

If the changed specimen were mated with a normal member of the species, the result would probably be seen in the next generation but one, the proportions being in accordance with Mendel's law. This, however, will be much more marked in the case of a deliberately changed specimen. Here is an example : Professor Guyer injected into a bird the substance from the lens of a rabbit's eye, thus obtaining an anti-lens serum. This he injected into a pregnant rabbit with the result that, although the mother's eyes remained unchanged, those of the young rabbits developed lenses that were in some way defective. On inbreeding among these offspring the defect would become inherited, even increased, after some generations. If, however, a defective rabbit were crossed with a normal one, the next generation in accordance with Mendel's law would all be normal, but in the third generation the defect would appear as a recessive Mendelian characteristic and would be passed on in accordance with the laws of Mendelian inheritance. Professor Guyer shows, too, that the defect can be inherited through either the male or the female parent, which means that the injection can take place before the embryo has come into being.

Now let us see how great are the "variations" brought about by chemical agency. Ever since the Devonian age vertebrata have had two eyes, and yet by adding a little chloride of magnesium to their water the eggs of certain fish have been made to develop into embryos with a single cyclopean eye in a median position.

I am interested in the texture—I use the word to denote general appearance of compactness, or otherwise—of the auras of people who are not of pure European strain. The aura of a Northern European is of fine texture by comparison with that of a negro, particularly the outer haze. The half-caste's aura is usually of a texture intermediate in appearance. This is the case, probably, no matter whether the individual resembles the white or the dark parent. One case in particular, that of a girl, aged twenty, blonde, with very pale complexion and bluish eyes. The father was also very fair and had exceptionally refined features—in fact, a typical specimen of the white man. The mother was dead, but it was rumoured that she had been a native of " some part of Africa." Apart from the fact that the girl had features somewhat on the coarse side, particularly the lips and nose, there was nothing in her appearance to support this rumour. A friend of mine was displaying interest in this girl and a member of his family had asked me whether there was any way of proving or disproving the ugly rumour about the girl's mother's origin without asking the father difficult questions and making things confoundedly awkward all round. An opportunity of inspecting this aura eventually presented itself. The texture was exceptionally coarse, so much so that to my mind there remained no shadow of doubt. Knowing the man's family, I had no hesitation in advising the man in the negative, as it were. I gave no reasons to him, but he took my advice which in itself showed that his infatuation must have been of a fleeting nature. Some years later this girl's brother returned from somewhere abroad. Clearly the aura had not lied, and things had turned out happily for all concerned, I am sure.

It is very rare that Mendel's law is carried out to the letter where human beings are concerned. The progeny of a black and white cross almost invariably results not in black or white individuals, but in darker or lighter brown ones. In the most exceptional case mentioned above, although the skin was white, the features were inherited from the maternal side. The characteristic black skin of the mother's race was present in that girl's make-up as a recessive characteristic; such presence could only be proved by the results of breeding, when it would be just as likely to assert itself, giving rise to a brown skin in the next generation, as if she had been herself dark skinned.

Mendel performed his original experiments with the flowers of peas. He crossed red with white with the result that the second generation so obtained were all pink. These pinks, crossed with one another, however, produced 25 per cent red which, crossed with other reds, bred true; 25 per cent white which, crossed with other whites, bred true, and 50 per cent pinks which were hybrids so far as colour was concerned. These intercrossed produced 25 per cent red which would never throw back;

25 per cent white which would never throw back, and 50 per cent hybrid pinks again.

He found the same rule to apply when a tall species of pea was crossed with a dwarf one. But, since there are no " middling-sized " peas, the second generation were all tall.

However, in the third generation 75 per cent were tall and 25 per cent dwarf. These dwarfs if self-fertilized or crossed with other dwarfs (in sweet peas self-fertilization is the rule) bred true. In the 75 per cent talls only 25 per cent if self-fertilized bred true to their type—viz. tall ; the other 50 per cent bred as hybrids— 25 per cent real talls ; 50 per cent talls but with hidden or recessive dwarf characteristics, and 25 per cent dwarfs.

Mendel explained his results by assuming that a characteristic may be dominant or recessive. Where both characteristics were present in the same plant the dominant type would prevail.

Let the tables overleaf explain themselves.

These hard and fast percentages are not adhered to in animals, much less in human beings, where the progeny is nearly always an intermediate. If, however, one parent is favoured outwardly, the characteristics of the other will be recessive.

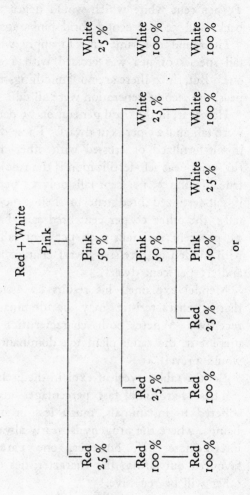

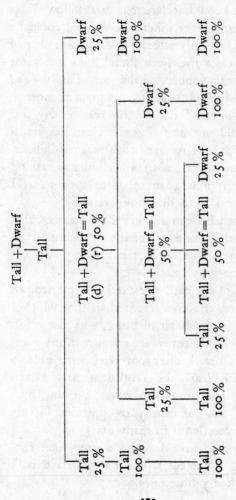

I wish I could declare that auras followed this Mendelian law of inheritance. That could be stated as fact only after a very great number of positive cases had been found among a great number of members of the same family—*and* similar results obtained from a great number of such families. I can see no reason why this law should not be followed. Here lies a real opportunity for research with real possibilities. To anybody who has an opportunity of making a study of a large number of such auras I recommend it to his consideration.

This much I can put on record, namely, that when both parents are of the intellectual type that possess blue auras, the progeny will not have ultra-grey ones.

Much of my earlier research was carried out with a less effective screen than that which I am now in the habit of using, with the result that I could not always see the aura in any great degree of detail, often not even being able to distinguish clearly the constituent parts. Given a correct background, however, the tint, blue or grey, was sufficiently recognizable for me to have recorded it in many cases.

In no case have I found a grey haze surrounding a subject whose parents have both had markedly blue ones.

Where one parent has been blue and the other grey, in each case to a marked degree, I have found that the children's auras have been either blue or blue-grey, very rarely dull grey. This shows that Mendel's law is not followed with regard to colour, the mean between extreme blue and extreme grey resulting with a tendency to improvement, which is what one would expect. Evolution must go on.

With texture Mendelian inheritance does seem to follow the rule more nearly, though there are exceptions. A fine texture mating with a coarse one appears to produce some fine, perhaps as fine as the fine parent ; some coarse, though not so coarse as the coarse parent, and the rest, the majority, betwixt-and-betweens.

Of the very few cases where I have had an opportunity of inspecting auras of three generations I have found that Mendel has had good support.

(1)

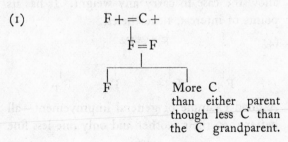

$$F + = C +$$
$$F = F$$

F   More C
           than either parent
           though less C than
           the C grandparent.

Another case in the same family :

(2)

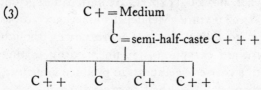

Much finer than either parent, though not quite up to the F grandparent, this third grandchild.

(3)

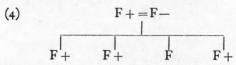

The second child, with the less elementary texture, so to speak, was, if anything, the darkest-skinned of the family. Incidentally the C+ grandparent was not too obviously European. In fact, a case where one needs to consider the generation earlier still if one is to allow the case to carry any weight. It has its points of interest, nevertheless.

(4)

$$F + = F -$$

$$F + \quad F + \quad F \quad F +$$

A good example of general improvement—all better than their mother and only one less fine in texture than the father, and, even so, definitely fine. Evolution goes on. Not always quite so boldly, though !

The colours tell much the same story in this case (4) :

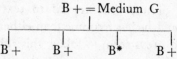

$$B + = \text{Medium } G$$

| B+ | B+ | B* | B+ |

* Nervy. With dorsal bulge—may improve.

The aura of the second child, B+ F+, is an exceptionally fine one, wide and bright.

The third may be described as having an " artistic temperament," but is generally considered to be " clever."

To return to the very depressing case (3), the question of colour hardly merits consideration. All, without exception, had dull grey auras with a suggestion of brown peculiar to coloured races, though only a suggestion of it. The negro aura is *always* coarse and of a very dull brownish grey.

In cases (1) and (2) the grandparents are the same and the middle generation are sisters ; both had medium blue auras. The grandchildren are very young still, though the (1) pair are, I think, both bluer than any of the (2) three. No test this, though.

Among cases in general, I feel that Mendel's law is applied rather more definitely with texture than as regards blues and greys. Mendel found that the next generation was intermediate, you will remember—half-way between the two parents. Thus, with regard to texture, the child should be less extreme than either parent. Blues and greys seem to follow this rule, too.

In the third generation, while the colours still tend to remain mixtures, the texture does quite decidedly throw back, viz. the younger child in case (1) and the third child in case (2). To form an opinion which would be of real value on this subject it would be necessary to have a record of the other grandparents, the parents of the second generation's mate. Possibly this individual may be a throwback ; by this I mean that the dominant characteristics may not represent a fair average of the joint texture of the parents. It must be remembered that recessive characteristics carry just as much weight in heredity as dominant ones do.

Take case (1) again :

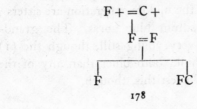

Suppose the other members of the second generation's mate had been on the coarse side, for example :

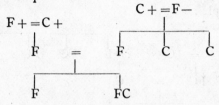

Then FC, instead of being considered below the family average, becomes rather above it, and the elder child of the third generation distinctly lucky. Yet the elder child is no more likely to produce finer textured progeny than the younger, for if the latter's aura shows a coarser texture as a dominant characteristic, the ability to pass on a finer textured aura such as that of the parents will be present as a recessive characteristic.

Similarly in case (2) :

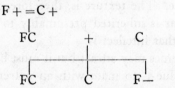

What do you suppose the auras of that second generation C were like ? Let us see what we can deduce.

Either they should have been coarse—or have averaged C, e.g. F=C+, or, if they averaged F, they, or one of them, was a throwback, for example :

F+ = C+   ?=F   FC   FC   C

      FC = C

      FC   C   F—

As I have said, much more evidence is required from many more cases before I should like to make a definite statement on the subject of inheritance of texture in auras, but there certainly does seem to be a Mendelian tendency. Quite decidedly a family that has had fine-textured auras for several generations will go on producing fine-textured auras. If there is no recessive C lying hidden, fine auras will continue. The texture is, therefore, inherited.

Colour is inherited presumably to the same extent that intellect is.

Extremes may attract but it must be unusual for a Blue+ to mate with an extreme Grey. Similarly, my example in cases (1) and (2), where the grandparents were extreme F and extreme C, is not to be met with every day.

Texture seems to be inherited and not acquired. I have not known a case where texture has undergone much change in a particular individual. Width and intensity will vary from time to time for reasons that have already been dealt with, but not texture nor appreciably colour. Shape of course will vary as mental health, and in the female with sexual changes ; there is no inheritance of shape except that the dorsal bulge will always be present in neurotic people—I suppose neurotic tendencies are inherited.

Now let me deal with two cases of twins. I had no opportunity of finding out anything about the grandparents in either case, nor even both parents in one.

Here is the first. Let us call it case (5). Twin girls—genuine twins.

Both parents had fine auras and fairly blue in colour.

Both children had auras identical in texture and so far as I could judge at their early age— they were just over a year old, when auras tend to be slightly green tinted—the colour was similar.

The outer haze in each case was of just the same width and shape, colour and texture, but the inside aura in the one case was more intense than in the other. The child with the brighter inside aura was undoubtedly the stronger twin. Since health in so young a baby is largely a question of digestion, I feel that this case is definitely helpful.

The other case—number (6)—was somewhat different. The twins were a boy and a girl. I did not know the mother at all, but the father was a very fine specimen of a man—a particularly lusty winging forward who weighed some sixteen stone of sheer muscle. His aura was bright, of fairly fine texture, somewhat on the grey side certainly, but decidedly a good, healthy aura.

The girl twin—their age was eight years when I looked at them—had a finer textured aura than her father's, and bluer. She was not strong physically and her inside aura was not particularly bright. The outer haze was not especially wide—it rarely is in children—and there was just a suggestion of a dorsal bulge. Not his very worst enemy could call her father neurotic or nervy. The child was rather that way inclined.

The boy was stronger physically ; his inside aura was brighter, while the outer haze was perhaps of slightly coarser texture and was definitely grey. No similarity at all between the auras of these twins.

If only it were possible to discover a means of making the aura more clearly visible I have but little doubt that we should find the auras differing greatly in classes of vertebrates, and quite distinctly in species, while even the auras of individuals would be dissimilar in some minor characteristics.

CHAPTER XIII

POSSIBILITIES

WILL any further headway be made along these lines of research?

It is difficult to say. Important discoveries are being made continually in other branches of science, some of which must have a bearing upon this work. To name only one that would entirely revolutionize present-day recognized views, oculists do not agree about the functions of the cones of the retina. Some think that they merely transmit stimulation in the retina to the optic nerve which leads direct to the brain. They appear to become shorter and fatter when light is acting upon them by drawing away from the pigment layer that lies beneath them, but lengthen out again to touch this layer when in darkness.

If the cells of the pigment layer move about, they could cause stimulation of the cones which may also be acted upon in some way chemically by the rhodopsin from the outer ends of the rods (the ends nearer to the sclerotic coat), for this becomes bleached in strong light, losing its purple colour. This suggests that we may have to attribute to the cones some prohibitive function, for they draw away from the pigment layer as if trying to put a stop to its stimulation of them.

This is only one of the suggested theories that may prove upsetting. Science is only now awakening. It was not many decades ago that we believed in spontaneous life—heaps of dead leaves turning into frogs, or clouds of dust into flies—and pumpkins into coaches! Views of this sort were given serious consideration right up till Darwin dropped his bombshell in the shape of *The Origin of Species*.

Again. Are we likely to be able to see more of the aura than has at present been seen?

Not until a more satisfactory means of translating the ultra-violet aura into something visible has been discovered. Here lies the next step and it is to this that research should be directed. I am not a chemist so can offer no useful suggestions.

What do I expect to find out further with regard to the aura?

I don't know what I should find, and really there seems to be no useful point to be gained by sheer guesswork—however, common sense surely suggests several lines of investigation. Since both parts of the aura have their origin from within the body and pass through the skin, the inside aura must overlap the wider haze in the vicinity of the body. I do not think that the actual particles that run to a magnet come through the skin from the endoderm, of course, but that part of the aura that is affected by disorders of the alimentary canal and its glands appears to extend as far from the skin as do these particles ; therefore I have treated this distance as the distal boundary of the inside aura. Here, at least, is its visible boundary.

The outer haze runs, in my opinion, intermingled with this though protruding much further from the body. The origin of this haze seems to be connected with the germinal layers, the mesoblast and the epiblast—viz. the mesoderm and the ectoderm. Now, I expect to find that the emissions are separate, and that these, too, are lying side by side. The part of the haze affected by the nervous system, that is to say the ectoderm part, I feel must extend considerably further than the elusive distal margin of the outer haze. Possibly the rays are of shorter wave-length and so are not rendered visible by my present screens, though changes in them can be appreciated while they run among the outer haze—which would then become the middle haze, since this outer invisible part would extend beyond it. So much points to the aura's extending considerably further than the distal margin as I have seen it, this distance being only about a foot in the best of subjects.

If this should prove to be the case, thought-transmission at once comes within the bounds of probability.

Kilner, as far away as the days before the War, speaks of an " extra outside aura." On the few occasions on which he saw it he treated it as an extension of the outer haze. It did not appear to indicate any symptoms in particular, but was faint. On one occasion, at least, he showed that it could be made brighter by a Wimshurst machine, but that it soon faded away and became unrecognizable.

I feel that this extra outer aura must always be present, but that its rays may have a wave-length lying *just* outside the sector of the spectrum rendered visible by the dye—I say " just " because to Kilner, who undoubtedly had an eye that was singularly gifted in some way, these rays occasionally became visible. Surely it was Kilner's eye and not the aura of the subject that caused them to be seen by him, or not to be seen.

I can offer no explanation for the extension or, rather, brightening of this distant haze when a Wimshurst was used. If I were to hazard a guess, it would seem that the material particles had been shot further afield so as to extend beyond the outer haze, but that on this occasion what he saw was not the extra outer aura at all.

All this, however, remains to be substantiated by experiment. Those long " searchlight " rays, too, will need to be further examined. Possibly the one may influence the other.

On two occasions only have I seen what I believe to be this third constituent part of the complete auric emission from the body. Obviously it would be ridiculous to draw definite conclusions from so little experience. I must needs find a method of enabling me to see this haze much more clearly before I can make any useful examination of it. I do feel, however, that it is present. I am sure what I saw was nothing subjective, no sort of illusion or phantom.

I have no sound reason for suggesting its origin as the ectoderm, except that I had been expecting to find a third, more distant haze, and that the nervous system seems the most likely source from my previous investigations. The change of shape of the outer haze, due to local extensions, has been of neural origin. You will remember the dorsal bulge which is most obvious and was dealt with at length by Kilner as long ago as the pre-War days. My screen has shown me more than I could ever hope to pick up with Kilner's dicyanin screen. This, let me point out with emphasis, is due not to me, but simply to the fact that Kilner must have done his work before the War, since his dye, to be obtained at its best (and nothing but the very best is any good for this work), comes from Germany. His eye was undoubtedly singularly gifted, but Science has marched on considerably since then. I consider that my screen portrays a clearer aura as well as extending its powers slightly further into the ultra-violet country.

Let us be frivolous for a moment and bring our imaginations with us for a conducted ramble into this exceedingly interesting country. We will keep in the sunshine, wave-length 400 $\mu\mu$ where the rainbow ends, to 310 $\mu\mu$ where is the frontier beyond which lies the dangerous abiotic realm. We must seek our aura between these limits ; I am not suggesting that we humans emit death rays, even to the destruction of the smallest creatures ; it is clear that we do not. As we leave the Rainbow land behind us we find it gets darker and darker, for here we can see only with our rods. Since the rods do not interpret reds at all yet see the other colours as blue-grey, it seems reasonable to suppose that we shall be able to use them while journeying through the ultra-violet red. Beyond this the rods may not help us, so this next colour to violet on the shorter side we may term the blue-grey band—which is lavender that needs brightening up. Thus I have referred to this red colour as lavender, because it appears as that colour to us—when we can see it. From here onwards we must use our screens if we are to see anything at all. I fancy we should have found most of our aura ere this, though I should not like to state this as a definite suggestion anywhere else—that was why I asked you to frivol. Let us go on a little further and seek the elusive third aura.

Only twice have I been here before so I fear I am a pretty useless guide. I do know that I have never been much further afield than this—if Kilner's extra-outer-aura on its non-electric occasions is to be identified in any way at all with what we seek—of which I cannot of course be sure, by any manner of means. We cannot go much further, though, for soon our country ends and we should then be out of the sun's limit and over into the abiotic land, which I feel would be a waste of time.

Let us navigate. Red's wave-length is 800 millimicrons; violet's is the octave of this, 400 $\mu\mu$. Visible red ends around 650, so we must now be getting out of the ultra-violet red region—and 310, or 300 at furthest, is our journey's end.

Our screens are by now not very helpful, and we are beginning to grope. Let us be turning home again. What have we discovered? Very little. These rays must be *about* half the length of visible red ones when they are beginning to merge into visible orange, viz. half 650 $\mu\mu$. Their frequency will be pretty terrific. The velocity of light is 186,000 miles per second. The velocity of sound in air is about 1100 feet per second—or 340 metres; I do not suppose 1100 feet quite matches 340 metres, and it matters not, since the velocity of sound will vary from time to time, of course. However, 340 metres are 340,000 millimetres. Velocity equals frequency multiplied by wave-length.

Therefore, frequency equals velocity divided

by wave-length, i.e. 340,000,000,000 millionths of a millimetre divided by about 310. Not a visible vibration, certainly !

In this lighter vein, on this note of catharsis, let us close these pages. Much remains to be done. This is a branch of science that offers great possibilities, there can be no doubt about that. If my modest attempt at collecting some facts and grouping them should prove a short cut to others who may care to travel a little further along what is at present untrodden bush, then this little book will perhaps have justified its inclusion in their bookshelves.

INDEX